THE BOOK OF
REVEL ATION
MADE CLEAR

THE BOOK OF
REVELATION
MADE CLEAR

A DOWN-TO-EARTH GUIDE
TO UNDERSTANDING THE MOST
MYSTERIOUS BOOK OF THE BIBLE

TIM LAHAYE &
TIMOTHY E. PARKER

NELSON
BOOKS
An Imprint of Thomas Nelson

Published in Nashville, Tennessee, by Nelson Books, an imprint of Thomas Nelson. Nelson Books and Thomas Nelson are registered trademarks of HarperCollins Christian Publishing, Inc.

Published in association with the literary agency of WordServe Literary Group, Ltd., www.wordserveliterary.com.

Published in association with the literary agency of Intellectual Property Group.

Thomas Nelson titles may be purchased in bulk for educational, business, fund-raising, or sales promotional use. For information, please e-mail SpecialMarkets@ThomasNelson.com.

Scripture quotations are taken from THE NEW KING JAMES VERSION. © 1982 by Thomas Nelson. Used by permission. All rights reserved.

ISBN: 978-0-5291-1690-1 (IE)

Library of Congress Cataloging-in-Publication Data

LaHaye, Tim F.
  The book of Revelation made clear : a down-to-earth guide to understanding the most mysterious book of the Bible / Tim LaHaye, Timothy E. Parker.
    pages cm
  Includes bibliographical references and index.
  ISBN 978-1-4002-0618-6 (alk. paper)
  1. Bible. Revelation--Textbooks. I. Title.
  BS2825.55.L34 2014
  228'.07--dc23

2013050886

Printed in the United States of America

23 24 25 26 27 LBC 20 19 18 17 16

To all who worship, admire, respect, fear, and love the Lord . . . and all those about to.

CONTENTS

INTRODUCTION

THE LORD'S LETTER

The book of Revelation is fascinating. While Genesis is the book of beginnings, Revelation is the book of completion. The sixty-sixth and final book of the Holy Bible, Revelation is unique in that it is the only New Testament book that centers primarily on future and prophetic events.

Revelation is widely believed to be the last of the sixty-six books of the Bible to be written. Using vibrant imagery, the book of Revelation describes the final victory of wise overcomers and the demise of the rebellious and disobedient. It describes the end of Satan and his eventual punishment in the lake of fire, and the unveiling of a new earth and a new heaven where death, suffering, crying, and pain will be no more.

Thirty years before the book of Revelation was written, Emperor Nero was engaged in the first organized, imperial persecution of Christians. Nero laughed at the screams of burning Christians, fed some to wild animals, crucified others, and generally made killing a sport, devising increasingly creative ways to slaughter men, women, and children. Both Peter and Paul suffered martyrdom at Nero's evil hands.

In AD 95, Titus Flavius Domitianus, commonly known as Domitian, was emperor of Rome. A ruthless ruler, he claimed to be a god and demanded all his subjects to worship him. When Christians refused, Domitian launched a campaign of persecution against them, especially the apostle John. Tens of thousands of Christians were tortured and killed under Domitian. After failing in an attempt to murder John by boiling him alive, Domitian banished him to the desolate, tiny, rocky island of Patmos, where John, alone with his difficulties, alone with his worship and with his thoughts, was given the revelation of Jesus Christ. It was there that he wrote the book of Revelation, describing the future and how the world will end.

Domitian's reign came to an end the very next year when he was assassinated by his own court officials. Upon his death, the Roman Senate condemned the memory of Domitian to oblivion.

How to Use This Book

This book is arranged strategically to provide the maximum potential for learning and retention. Every verse of Revelation is covered, and the entire book is explained in a specific way.

Each section begins with a short pre-quiz. Please attempt to answer the three multiple-choice questions, whether you believe you know them already or not. The questions are followed by the scripture that pertains to them, and then a precise explanation of what the scripture means.

Finally, the same three questions are repeated, but with the answers provided.

By following this method, you will be amazed at how well you retain the teachings. You will most likely be able to review the quizzes months, even years later and still know the answers.

The book of Revelation promises a blessing to anyone who reads it and takes it to heart, so by merely completing this book, you'll be halfway to your blessing from the Lord Most High.

REVELATION

1

THE BLESSING BEGINS

📖 REVELATION 1:1–2

Pre-Quiz

1. The book of Revelation concerns God's disclosures of future events through the visions and symbols of
   A. Elijah
   B. Jesus Christ
   C. Paul

2. The purpose of the revelation is to
   A. review all things the Lord has done
   B. show which things must shortly come to pass
   C. show what needs to be changed on the earth

3. Who was inspired by God to write the book of Revelation?
   A. Moses
   B. Paul
   C. John

What the Scriptures Say (Revelation 1:1–2)

The Revelation of Jesus Christ, which God gave Him to show His servants—things which must shortly take place. And He sent and signified it by His angel to His servant John, who bore witness to the word of God, and to the testimony of Jesus Christ, to all things that he saw.

What Revelation 1:1–2 Means

The "Him" in this verse is Jesus Christ. The Father gave the revelation to Jesus, Jesus then gave the revelation to John, and John gave the revelation to us.

QUICK FACT: Verse 1 includes the segment "things which must shortly take place." Revelation was written in Greek. The Greek translation of *shortly* is *en tachei*, which means "great rapidity." The word *tachometer*, referring to the dashboard aid that measures engine speed, is derived from *en tachei*. Despite Revelation being written almost two thousand years ago, to God the prophecies of the book will happen with "great rapidity."

Revelation 1:1–2 Quiz Answers

1. The book of Revelation concerns God's disclosures of future events through the visions and symbols of B) Jesus Christ.
2. The purpose of the revelation is to B) show which things must shortly come to pass.
3. Who was inspired by God to write the book of Revelation? C) John

📖 REVELATION 1:3

Pre-Quiz

1. Who does Revelation claim will receive a blessing?
   A. everyone
   B. whoever reads Revelation and takes it to heart
   C. no one in particular

2. Not only must one hear the words of prophecy, but one must also
   A. perform works
   B. take the prophecies to heart
   C. make prophecies of one's own

3. What is the dire warning at the end of Revelation 1:3?
   A. The apocalypse is happening now.
   B. There will be no more warnings.
   C. The time is near.

What the Scriptures Say (Revelation 1:3)

Blessed is he who reads and those who hear the words of this prophecy, and keep those things which are written in it; for the time is near.

What Revelation 1:3 Means

This is a clear and unmistakable promise from God. It contains no hint of parable or symbology. This is a direct promise that anyone is blessed who reads and hears the words of this prophecy and who keeps the things written in it.

Revelation 1:3 Quiz Answers

1. Who does Revelation proclaim will receive a blessing? B) whoever reads Revelation and takes it to heart

2. Not only must one hear the words of prophecy, but one must also B) take the prophecies to heart.

3. What is the dire warning at the end of Revelation 1:3? C) The time is near.

📖 REVELATION 1:4–5

Pre-Quiz

1. Who is John writing the book of Revelation to?
   A. seven churches in Asia
   B. anyone within earshot
   C. Jesus

2. How many spirits are there before the throne?
   A. one
   B. three
   C. seven

3. Who is called the firstborn of the dead?
   A. Lazarus
   B. John
   C. Jesus

What the Scriptures Say (Revelation 1:4–5)

John, to the seven churches which are in Asia: Grace to you and peace from Him who is and who was and who is to come, and from the seven Spirits who are before His throne, and from Jesus Christ, the faithful witness, the firstborn from the dead, and the ruler over the kings of the earth. To Him who loved us and washed us from our sins in His own blood, . . .

What Revelation 1:4–5 Means

These verses contain John's greeting in his letter to the seven churches. The greeting was included along with a copy of the prophecy, a cover letter explaining how he received the prophecy and why he was sending it out.

The instructions for each church come directly from Jesus. Revelation 2–3 covers Jesus' actual instructions.

The "Asia" mentioned in verse 4 is not our modern-day Asia. It refers to modern-day Turkey.

The seven spirits mentioned in verse 4 refer to the sevenfold ministry of the Holy Spirit. This is confirmed in Isaiah 11:2: "The Spirit of the LORD [1] shall rest upon Him, the Spirit of wisdom [2] and understanding, [3] the Spirit of counsel [4] and might, [5] the Spirit of knowledge [6] and of the fear of the LORD [7]."

Revelation 1:4–5 Quiz Answers

1. Who is John writing the book of Revelation to? A) seven churches in Asia
2. How many spirits are there before the throne? C) seven
3. Who is called the firstborn of the dead? C) Jesus

QUICK FACT: The book of Revelation is the only book of the Bible that offers a blessing to anyone reading it aloud or hearing it read.

📖 Revelation 1:6–7

Pre-Quiz

1. What are we made unto God (Jesus) and His Father?
   A. kings and princes
   B. the righteous
   C. kings and priests

2. According to Revelation 1:7, when Jesus comes back among the clouds, everyone will see Him, including
   A. the blind
   B. those who pierced Him
   C. those who rejected Him

3. And all the earth shall do what because of Him?
   A. laugh with joy
   B. mourn
   C. be caught up in the sky

What the Scriptures Say (Revelation 1:6–7)

. . . and has made us kings and priests to His God and Father, to Him be glory and dominion forever and ever. Amen. Behold, He is coming with clouds, and every eye will see Him, even they who pierced Him. And all the tribes of the earth will mourn because of Him. Even so, Amen.

What Revelation 1:6–7 Means

"Coming with clouds" echoes the vision of Daniel in Daniel 7:13: "I was watching in the night visions, and behold, One like the Son of Man, coming with the clouds of heaven! He came to the Ancient of Days, and they brought Him near before Him."

"Every eye will see Him" means exactly that. At the second coming of Christ, all will see Him. "Pierced Him" refers to the crucifixion of Christ. Those who didn't believe in Christ will "mourn" with regret over their disbelief.

Revelation 1:6–7 Quiz Answers

1. What are we made unto God (Jesus) and His Father? C) kings and priests
2. According to Revelation 1:7, when Jesus comes back among the clouds, everyone will see Him, including B) those who pierced Him.
3. And all the earth shall do what because of Him? B) mourn

📖 REVELATION 1:8–10

Pre-Quiz
1. "I am the Alpha and Omega" means Jesus is the
    A. heads and the tails
    B. Beginning and the End
    C. front and the back

2. John claims to be our brother and companion in
    A. faith
    B. tribulation
    C. prayer

3. While in the Spirit, John heard a great voice that sounded like a
    A. trumpet
    B. harp
    C. roaring lion

What the Scriptures Say (Revelation 1:8)

"I am the Alpha and the Omega, the Beginning and the End," says the Lord, "who is and who was and who is to come, the Almighty."

What Revelation 1:8 Means

God describes Himself as "the Alpha and the Omega." These are the first and last letters of the Greek alphabet and signify that God is almighty from beginning to end, encompassing everything in between.

What the Scriptures Say (Revelation 1:9)

I, John, both your brother and companion in the tribulation and kingdom and patience of Jesus Christ, was on the island that is called Patmos for the word of God and for the testimony of Jesus Christ.

What Revelation 1:9 Means

By describing himself as a "brother and companion in the tribulation," John is humanizing himself as one going through the trials and tribulations of others. He is careful not to exalt himself over anyone, and he is clearly signaling that he himself is not divine, but merely a human messenger of God. John's use of the word *tribulation* is in line with Paul and Barnabas's observance in Acts 14:22: "Strengthening the souls of the disciples, exhorting them to continue in the faith, and saying, 'We must through many tribulations enter the kingdom of God.'"

What the Scriptures Say (Revelation 1:10)

> I was in the Spirit on the Lord's Day, and I heard behind me a loud voice, as of a trumpet . . .

What Revelation 1:10 Means

"In the Spirit" expresses John's desire to ensure that he was not day-dreaming or imagining things as a human might, but was under the influence of spiritual guidance, perhaps deep in prayer, but certainly in communication with God when he heard a "loud voice."

The "Lord's Day," consistently throughout the Bible, is the first day of the week. Under the old covenant, the seventh day of the week, Saturday, was the Sabbath.

When John wrote, "and I heard behind me a loud voice, as of a trumpet," a similarity to the apostle Paul's letter to the Thessalonians is evident. "For the Lord Himself will descend from heaven with a shout, with the voice of an archangel, and with the trumpet of God. And the dead in Christ will rise first" (1 Thess. 4:16).

Revelation 1:8–10 Quiz Answers

1. "I am the Alpha and the Omega" means Jesus is the B) Beginning and the End.
2. John claims to be our brother and companion in B) tribulation.
3. While in the Spirit, John heard a great voice that sounded like a A) trumpet.

📖 REVELATION 1:11–13

Pre-Quiz

1. Which was the first church to receive John's letter?
   A. Ephesus
   B. Pergamum
   C. Thyatira

2. When John turned in the direction of the voice he heard, what did he see?
   A. the angel of the Lord
   B. seven golden lampstands
   C. the heavenly gates

3. Who was wearing a garment "down to the feet"?
   A. John
   B. the prophet of old
   C. the Son of Man

What the Scriptures Say (Revelation 1:11)

. . . saying, "I am the Alpha and the Omega, the First and the Last," and, "What you see, write in a book and send it to the seven churches which are in Asia: to Ephesus, to Smyrna, to Pergamos, to Thyatira, to Sardis, to Philadelphia, and to Laodicea."

What Revelation 1:11 Means

Each of the seven churches received the entire book of Revelation, and as we find out in Revelation 2:1, each also received a letter from Jesus Christ.

What the Scriptures Say (Revelation 1:12–13)

Then I turned to see the voice that spoke with me. And having turned I saw seven golden lampstands, and in the midst of the seven lampstands One like the Son of Man, clothed with a garment down to the feet and girded about the chest with a golden band.

What Revelation 1:12–13 Means

The voice that spoke to John was that of Jesus Christ. The "seven lamp-stands" is <u>the first of twenty-one symbols used in the book of Revelation</u> and represents the seven churches. The King James Version calls them "candlesticks" in this verse.

"The Son of Man" is Jesus Christ. A cross-reference to "Son of Man" occurs in Daniel 7:13: "I was watching in the night visions, and behold, One like the Son of Man, coming with the clouds of heaven! He came to the Ancient of Days, and they brought Him near before Him."

Jesus is dressed in the manner of the high priests of the Old Testament with a "garment down to the feet" and a "golden band" around His chest. This is confirmed in Daniel 10:5–6, which remarkably has a very similar description: "I lifted my eyes and looked, and behold, a certain man clothed in linen, whose waist was girded with gold of Uphaz! His body was like beryl, his face like the appearance of lightning, his eyes like torches of fire, his arms and feet like burnished bronze in color, and the sound of his words like the voice of a multitude."

There is no doubt that it is Jesus whom John sees.

Revelation 1:11–13 Quiz Answers

1. Which was the first church to receive John's letter? A) Ephesus
2. When John turned in the direction of the voice he heard, what did he see? B) seven golden lampstands
3. Who was wearing a garment "down to the feet"? C) the Son of Man

📖 REVELATION 1:14–15

Pre-Quiz

1. How did John describe Jesus' hair?
   A. as flowing locks
   B. as white wool
   C. as bronze

2. How did John describe Jesus' eyes?
   A. as bright as the sun
   B. as a flame of fire
   C. as powerful as thunder

3. Jesus' feet are described as fine brass and His voice as
   A. the roar of a waterfall
   B. the voice of many waters
   C. the blare of a trumpet

What the Scriptures Say (Revelation 1:14)

His head and hair were white like wool, as white as snow, and His eyes like a flame of fire.

What Revelation 1:14 Means

The color white is very significant. It represents purity, and the use of white in the description of Jesus corresponds directly and forcefully to the Old Testament description in Daniel 7:9: "I watched till thrones were put in place, and the Ancient of Days was seated; His garment was white as snow, and the hair of His head was like pure wool. His throne was a fiery flame, its wheels a burning fire."

Another strong correlation occurs in Matthew 17:2 concerning Jesus Christ on the Mount of Transfiguration: "and He was transfigured before them. His face shone like the sun, and His clothes became as white as the light."

What the Scriptures Say (Revelation 1:15)

His feet were like fine brass, as if refined in a furnace, and His voice as the sound of many waters.

What Revelation 1:15 Means

"Feet . . . like fine brass" symbolizes Jesus' ability to trample anything underfoot. *Fine* means "rubbed and polished," an indication that Jesus has overcome His earthly trials of the Gospels. He is now a polished conqueror, a warrior of the highest order. In addition, Jesus' feet being compared to "fine brass" symbolizes divine wisdom and judgment.

In Exodus 38:30, "And with it he made the sockets for the door of the tabernacle of meeting, the bronze altar, the bronze grating for it, and all the utensils for the altar," the use of brass (as in "bronze altar" and "bronze grating") is associated with sin sacrifices.

His voice "of many waters" signifies a power and authority, as that of the roar of a mighty waterfall. Psalm 93:4 states, "The LORD on high is mightier than the noise of many waters, than the mighty waves of the sea."

Revelation 1:14–15 Quiz Answers
1. How did John describe Jesus' hair? B) as white wool
2. How did John describe Jesus' eyes? B) as a flame of fire
3. Jesus' feet are described as fine brass and His voice as B) the voice of many waters.

📖 REVELATION 1:16–17

Pre-Quiz
1. What was Jesus holding in His right hand?
   A. seven stars
   B. seven candles
   C. seven bolts of lightning

2. What was Jesus' countenance (appearance) compared to?
   A. the sun
   B. stars in heaven
   C. the universe

3. What did John do when he saw Jesus arrayed this way?
   A. He fell dead at His feet (fainted).
   B. He became caught up in the spirit.
   C. He was temporarily blinded.

What the Scriptures Say (Revelation 1:16)

He had in His right hand seven stars, out of His mouth went a sharp two-edged sword, and His countenance was like the sun shining in its strength.

What Revelation 1:16 Means

The "seven stars" in Jesus' right hand is the second of twenty-one symbols used in the book of Revelation. The "two-edged" sword is the third symbol.

The two-edged sword is used in Hebrews 4:12 in a comparison to God's Word: "For the word of God is living and powerful, and sharper than any two-edged sword, piercing even to the division of soul and spirit, and of joints and marrow, and is a discerner of the thoughts and intents of the heart."

The "seven stars" will be explained in verse 20 as representing "the angels of the seven churches," and their being in Jesus' right hand is a powerful statement that brings to mind what Jesus said in John 10:27–28: "My sheep hear My voice, and I know them, and they follow Me. And I give them eternal life, and they shall never perish; neither shall anyone snatch them out of My hand."

What the Scriptures Say (Revelation 1:17)

And when I saw Him, I fell at His feet as dead. But He laid His right hand on me, saying to me, "Do not be afraid; I am the First and the Last."

What Revelation 1:17 Means

John's overwhelming reaction to seeing Jesus has a twin account in Daniel 10:9: "Yet I heard the sound of his words; and while I heard the sound of his words I was in a deep sleep on my face, with my face to the ground."

Revelation 1:16–17 Quiz Answers

1. What was Jesus holding in His right hand? A) seven stars
2. What was Jesus' countenance (appearance) compared to? A) the sun
3. What did John do when he saw Jesus arrayed this way? A) He fell dead at His feet (fainted).

📖 REVELATION 1:18–20

Pre-Quiz

1. What did Jesus proclaim He held the keys to?
   A. the universe
   B. the gates of heaven
   C. Hades and death

2. Jesus told John to write things of
   A. the future only
   B. the past
   C. the past, present, and future

3. Jesus confirmed the seven stars in His right hand were the
   A. seven churches
   B. seven torches
   C. seven angels of the seven churches

What the Scriptures Say (Revelation 1:18)

"I am He who lives, and was dead, and behold, I am alive forevermore. Amen. And I have the keys of Hades and of Death."

What Revelation 1:18 Means

Christ verifies His eternal existence, referencing His crucifixion and resurrection. Romans 6:9 declares: "Knowing that Christ, having been raised from the dead, dies no more. Death no longer has dominion over Him."

What the Scriptures Say (Revelation 1:19)

"Write the things which you have seen, and the things which are, and the things which will take place after this."

What Revelation 1:19 Means

John is instructed in how to map out the book of Revelation, including John's eyewitness accounts.

What the Scriptures Say (Revelation 1:20)

"The mystery of the seven stars which you saw in My right hand, and the seven golden lampstands: The seven stars are the angels of the seven churches, and the seven lampstands which you saw are the seven churches."

What Revelation 1:20 Means

There is no reason to suggest the "angels of the seven churches" are anything other than actual angels—supernatural beings. Since Revelation 5:2 refers to a supernatural angel, it is wise to view the angels of the seven churches as actual, supernatural beings as well.

Revelation 1:18–20 Quiz Answers

1. What did Jesus proclaim He held the keys to? C) Hades and death
2. Jesus told John to write things of C) the past, present, and future.
3. Jesus confirmed the seven stars in His right hand were the C) seven angels of the seven churches.

MORE QUICK FACTS ON THE SEVEN CHURCHES

- The church in Smyrna and the church in Philadelphia were considered to be very good churches. They were mainly composed of a heavily persecuted, humble class of people.
- The church in Pergamum believed in Christ, but openly permitted other pagan doctrines full of opinions and interpretations that sometimes went against the very nature of Christ.

- The church in Ephesus was very strict in its teachings, but was falling away from Jesus and His teachings.
- The church in Thyatira was zealous and enthusiastic, but still permitted Jezebel's heresy.
- The church in Laodicea and the church in Sardis had memberships composed mostly of the ruling class and were thoroughly pagan in nature. There was a hint of belief in Christ, but the belief was not followed with Christlike lifestyles.

REVELATION

THE CHURCHES

📖 **REVELATION 2:1–5**

Pre-Quiz

1. Who is speaking as chapter 2 begins?
   A. John
   B. the angel of the Lord
   C. Jesus

2. In Revelation 2:4, what does Jesus say they had left?
   A. your first love
   B. your faith
   C. your tribulations

3. Jesus states that He will come unto you
   A. as a thief in the night
   B. quickly
   C. before you can blink an eye

What the Scriptures Say (Revelation 2:1–2)

"To the angel of the church of Ephesus write, 'These things says He who holds the seven stars in His right hand, who walks in the midst of the seven golden lampstands: "I know your works, your labor, your patience, and that you cannot bear those who are evil. And you have tested those who say they are apostles and are not, and have found them liars."'"

What Revelation 2:1–2 Means

The seven churches of Revelation were representative of all churches of the time. Some were strong in their faith, some so-so, and some were woefully deficient.

Ephesus was a major metropolis. It was the primary commercial center of Asia Minor, and the temple of Artemis in Ephesus was one of the Seven Wonders of the Ancient World. It was in Ephesus that Paul led many to Christ, and the church had grown into a powerhouse. Ephesus was also the location of Timothy's martyrdom under Emperor Domitian.

As Jesus addresses each of the churches, He begins by pointing out positive traits that are pleasing to Him, followed by what displeases Him. He asserts the fact that He is all-knowing with His statement in verse 2, "I know your works . . ."

What the Scriptures Say (Revelation 2:3–4)

" . . . and you have persevered and have patience, and have labored for My name's sake and have not become weary. Nevertheless I have this against you, that you have left your first love."

What Revelation 2:3–4 Means

Leaving the "first love" of the church means a diminishing of the initial zeal the church had for the Lord and His ways. Though Jesus states He is against the church for drifting, as is characteristic of the love of Christ, He is still there, supportive and ready to forgive.

It is also significant that Jesus says the church has "left" its first love rather than "lost" its first love, signaling the opportunity for the church to return to its original spirituality.

What the Scriptures Say (Revelation 2:5)

"Remember therefore from where you have fallen; repent and do the first works, or else I will come to you quickly and remove your lampstand from its place—unless you repent."

What Revelation 2:5 Means

Jesus is advising the church to remember its initial enthusiasm when it put Christ first. He urges it to repent and go back to the church's first works. "Remove your lampstand" means to place judgment on the church and remove its representation at the throne of God.

Notice that Jesus uses the word *quickly*. This urgency gives His warning added significance.

Revelation 2:1–5 Quiz Answers

1. Who is speaking as chapter 2 begins? C) Jesus
2. In Revelation 2:4, what does Jesus say they had left? A) your first love
3. Jesus states that He will come unto you B) quickly.

📖 REVELATION 2:6–10

Pre-Quiz

1. In Revelation 2:6, whose deeds did Jesus say He hates?
   A. the Nicolaitans
   B. sinners
   C. the church in Smyrna

2. Who would eat of the tree in the midst of paradise?
   A. all who believe
   B. he who overcomes
   C. any and everyone

3. The church of Smyrna was told some of them would be thrown in
   prison by
   A. unbelievers
   B. Satan
   C. blasphemers

What the Scriptures Say (Revelation 2:6)

"But this you have, that you hate the deeds of the Nicolaitans, which I also hate."

What Revelation 2:6 Means

Although not entirely pleased with the Ephesian church, Jesus commends it for despising the deeds of the Nicolaitans. The Nicolaitans were known for having devious lifestyles. They were greedy and had false teachers among them. Jesus didn't hate the individuals, but He did hate their deeds.

What the Scriptures Say (Revelation 2:7)

"He who has an ear, let him hear what the Spirit says to the churches. To him who overcomes I will give to eat from the tree of life, which is in the midst of the Paradise of God."

What Revelation 2:7 Means

Here, Jesus is calling for repentance. Anyone who overcomes is victorious. But the book of John gives us the definition of an overcomer. In 1 John 5:4–5, John defines a victorious one as a believer in Christ. When Jesus states in this verse, "I will give to eat from the tree of life," He is referring to eternal life.

What the Scriptures Say (Revelation 2:8)

"And to the angel of the church in Smyrna write, 'These things says the First and the Last, who was dead, and came to life.'"

What Revelation 2:8 Means

Smyrna was a major seaport. It was an industrial center known for making wine. It was dotted with many temples, with one dedicated to Emperor Tiberius. The people of the church were basically poor. Yet, there was no rebuke from Jesus for the church. Instead, Jesus extends comfort and support.

The Christian believers there were persecuted because of the menacing presence of the Romans and a large Jewish population. Because of heavy persecution, many were killed and many others became martyrs. This explains Jesus' reassurance that He is the One who died and lived, giving hope to the church through eternal life.

The church in Smyrna and the church in Philadelphia were not rebuked by Jesus. "And to the angel of the church in Smyrna" means "to the messenger of the church in Smyrna." The messenger is not an actual angel, but a human messenger.

What the Scriptures Say (Revelation 2:9)

"I know your works, tribulation, and poverty (but you are rich); and I know the blasphemy of those who say they are Jews and are not, but are a synagogue of Satan."

What Revelation 2:9 Means

When Jesus tells the church that it is rich, He means spiritually rich. The Jews whom Jesus refers to are a particular group of apostate (one who forsakes his religion) Jews. These particular Jews were used by Satan as the chief persecutors. Historically, an example occurred in AD 155 when Polycarp, a Christian bishop of Smyrna, was martyred. Many apostate Jews assisted in his killing by gathering wood on the Sabbath for the fire upon which Polycarp was burned to death.

What the Scriptures Say (Revelation 2:10)

"Do not fear any of those things which you are about to suffer. Indeed, the devil is about to throw some of you into prison, that you may be tested, and you will have tribulation ten days. Be faithful until death, and I will give you the crown of life."

What Revelation 2:10 Means

The ten tribulation days are actual days. The crown of life, which is also referred to in James 1:12, is a prize for believers who persevere.

Revelation 2:6–10 Quiz Answers

1. In Revelation 2:6, whose deeds did Jesus say He hates? A) the Nicolaitans
2. Who would eat of the tree in the midst of paradise? B) he who overcomes
3. The church of Smyrna was told some of them would be thrown in prison by B) Satan.

📖 REVELATION 2:11–14

Pre-Quiz

1. Jesus says that he who overcomes shall not be hurt by the second
   A. death
   B. wind
   C. coming

2. Who did Jesus call this faithful martyr?
   A. John
   B. Stephen
   C. Antipas

3. Jesus accused the church of Pergamos of holding to the doctrine of
   A. Balaam
   B. Satan
   C. no one

What the Scriptures Say (Revelation 2:11)

"He who has an ear, let him hear what the Spirit says to the churches. He who overcomes shall not be hurt by the second death."

What Revelation 2:11 Means

He who overcomes will have everlasting life with God. To die a "second death" means being delivered from the judgment throne that leads to hell.

What the Scriptures Say (Revelation 2:12–14)

"And to the angel of the church in Pergamos write, 'These things says He who has the sharp two-edged sword: "I know your works, and where you dwell, where Satan's throne is. And you hold fast to My name, and did not deny My faith even in the days in which Antipas was My faithful martyr, who was killed among you, where Satan dwells. But I have a few things against you, because you have there those who hold the doctrine of Balaam, who taught Balak to put a stumbling block before the children of Israel, to eat things sacrificed to idols, and to commit sexual immorality."'"

What Revelation 2:12–14 Means

"To the angel of the church in Pergamos" means "to the messenger of the church."

Revelation 2:11–14 Quiz Answers

1. Jesus says that he who overcomes shall not be hurt by the second A) death.
2. Who did Jesus call this faithful martyr? C) Antipas
3. Jesus accused the church of Pergamos of holding to the doctrine of A) Balaam.

📖 REVELATION 2:15–17

Pre-Quiz

1. What does Jesus command the church of Pergamos to do?
   A. return to its first love
   B. repent
   C. prepare for battle

2. What food is offered to those who overcome?
   A. milk and honey
   B. manna
   C. the fruit of the land

3. When Jesus mentions a white stone, what does He say will be written on it?
   A. a new name
   B. the book of Revelation
   C. the names of those given eternal life

What the Scriptures Say (Revelation 2:15–17)

"Thus you also have those who hold the doctrine of the Nicolaitans, which thing I hate. Repent, or else I will come to you quickly and will fight against them with the sword of My mouth. He who has an ear, let him hear what the Spirit says to the churches. To him who overcomes I will give some of the hidden manna to eat. And I will give him a white stone, and on the stone a new name written which no one knows except him who receives it."

What Revelation 2:15–17 Means

Jesus reveals His hatred for immorality. The purity of Jesus' doctrine cannot and should not be changed or compromised to appear more acceptable politically or socially.

Jesus promises to fulfill the needs of His faithful followers.

Revelation 2:15–17 Quiz Answers

1. What does Jesus command the church of Pergamos to do? B) repent
2. What food is offered to those who overcome? B) manna
3. When Jesus mentions a white stone, what does He say will be written on it? A) a new name

📖 REVELATION 2:18–23

Pre-Quiz

1. Jesus accused the church in Thyatira of allowing Jezebel to teach His servants to
   A. commit sexual immorality
   B. work on the Sabbath
   C. ignore the Commandments

2. Who did Jesus threaten to cast into a sickbed?
   A. sinners
   B. Jezebel
   C. false prophets

3. Jesus said, "I will give to each one of you according to your _____."
   A. works
   B. riches
   C. gifts

What the Scriptures Say (Revelation 2:18–23)

"And to the angel of the church in Thyatira write, 'These things says the Son of God, who has eyes like a flame of fire, and His feet like fine brass: "I know your works, love, service, faith, and your patience; and as for your works, the last are more than the first. Nevertheless I have a few things against you, because you allow that woman Jezebel, who calls herself a prophetess, to teach and seduce My servants to commit sexual immorality and eat things sacrificed to idols. And I gave her time to repent of her sexual immorality, and she did not repent. Indeed I will cast her into a sickbed, and those who commit adultery with her into great tribulation, unless they repent of their deeds. I will kill her children with death, and all the churches shall know that I am He who searches the minds and hearts. And I will give to each one of you according to your works.""'"

What Revelation 2:18–23 Means

Thyatira was an industrious city with a large military presence. It was located about thirty miles south from Pergamos and was a major producer of wool and dye.

"To the angel of the church" means "to the messenger of the church."

This third letter to the seven churches is identified as being a message from Jesus, as it follows the same pattern as the others. It contains what Jesus knew was commendable about the church, followed by what displeases Him. Jesus would then offer a solution to what displeases Him, and call for genuine repentance.

Jesus describes Himself to the church in Thyatira as having "eyes like a flame of fire, and His feet like fine brass." Daniel 10:6 gives us a nearly identical description of Christ: "His body was like beryl, his face like the appearance of lightning, his eyes like torches of fire, his arms and feet like burnished bronze in color, and the sound of his words like the voice of a multitude."

Jesus has a severe problem with a woman named Jezebel. This is not the same Jezebel from the Old Testament, Queen Jezebel of 1 and 2 Kings. She is a New Testament woman who had a huge following in Thyatira.

Note that Jesus says, "who calls herself a prophetess." This clearly indicates that Jezebel is only a prophetess in her own mind. Jesus does not call her a prophetess, nor does He call her to be one. She calls herself a prophetess.

Claiming to be inspired by God, Jezebel taught her followers in the church in Thyatira profane teachings in the eyes of God. In verse 21, Jesus reveals that He was patient with her, allowing her time to repent, but she did not seize the opportunity and continued with her false doctrine.

Verse 22 includes a dire warning to all false teachers, false prophets, and others who damage God's church. Jesus allows opportunity for genuine repentance, but if change is not forthcoming, then Jesus, in protecting His church, will deal out severe punishment to offenders.

Ezekiel 13:19–21 gives a similar warning, displaying the extreme distaste Jesus has for false teachings: "'And will you profane Me among My people for handfuls of barley and for pieces of bread, killing people who should not die, and keeping people alive who should not live, by your lying to My people who listen to lies?' Therefore thus says the Lord GOD: 'Behold, I am against your magic charms by which you hunt souls there like birds. I will tear them from your arms, and let the souls go, the souls you hunt like birds. I will also tear off your veils and deliver My people out of your hand, and they shall no longer be as prey in your hand. Then you shall know that I am the LORD.'"

In verse 23, Jesus threatens Jezebel's "children." The children are her followers, not necessarily her birth children, although if she had any, they would be included among that number if they followed her teachings as well. Jesus is quite clear that He will kill her followers. There is no indication that this is a spiritual death.

The end of verse 23 reads, "I will give to each one of you according to your works." This is mirrored in the Old Testament in Psalm 62:12: "Also to You, O Lord, belongs mercy; for You render to each one according to his work."

Revelation 2:18–23 Quiz Answers
1. Jesus accused the church in Thyatira of allowing Jezebel to teach His servants to A) commit sexual immorality.
2. Who did Jesus threaten to cast into a sickbed? B) Jezebel
3. Jesus said, "I will give to each one of you according to your _____." A) works

📖 REVELATION 2:24–29

Pre-Quiz

1. The church in Thyatira was told that it does not know the depths of
   A. despair
   B. Satan
   C. God's love

2. To him who overcomes and keeps Jesus' works to the end, will be given
   A. power over the nations
   B. power over himself
   C. power over others

3. What will be broken into pieces?
   A. the will of the enemy
   B. the last nation standing
   C. the vessels of a potter

What the Scriptures Say (Revelation 2:24–29)

"Now to you I say, and to the rest in Thyatira, as many as do not have this doctrine, who have not known the depths of Satan, as they say, I will put on you no other burden. But hold fast what you have till I come. And he who overcomes, and keeps My works until the end, to him I will give power over the nations—

'He shall rule them with a rod of iron;
They shall be dashed to pieces like the potter's vessels'—

as I also have received from My Father; and I will give him the morning star.

He who has an ear, let him hear what the Spirit says to the churches."

What Revelation 2:24–29 Means

Fortunately, there were many in the church in Thyatira who rejected the teachings of Jezebel. Jesus promises not to put the same burden on them that will be put on Jezebel's true followers.

As He does in all His letters, Jesus has a word to the overcomer. The overcomer is obedient and faithful to Christ's teachings. Jesus' promise to give great power to the overcomer is available to anyone obedient to His commands to the end—a faithful follower. "Until the end" is the disclaimer. Many may fall short or grow weary, but it is the persistent one who gains the promise of the power.

There is a very similar passage referencing the power given to the overcomer in Psalm 2:8–9: "Ask of Me, and I will give You the nations for Your inheritance, and the ends of the earth for Your possession. You shall break them with a rod of iron; You shall dash them to pieces like a potter's vessel."

Revelation 2:24–29 Quiz Answers

1. The church in Thyatira was told that it does not know the depths of B) Satan.
2. To him who overcomes and keeps Jesus' works to the end, will be given A) power over the nations.
3. What will be broken into pieces? C) the vessels of a potter

REVELATION

SPIRITUAL DEATHS

📖 REVELATION 3:1–4

Pre-Quiz

1. Jesus said that the church in Sardis is
   A. alive
   B. thriving
   C. dead

2. Jesus told the church to hold fast and
   A. pray
   B. repent
   C. fight

3. The church in Sardis was told that they have but a few names who have not defiled their
   A. souls
   B. garments
   C. church

What the Scriptures Say (Revelation 3:1–4)

"And to the angel of the church in Sardis write, 'These things says He who has the seven Spirits of God and the seven stars: "I know your works, that you have a name that you are alive, but you are dead. Be watchful, and strengthen the things which remain, that are ready to die, for I have not found your works perfect before God. Remember therefore how you have received and heard; hold fast and repent. Therefore if you will not watch, I will come upon you as a thief, and you will not know what hour I will come upon you. You have a few names even in Sardis who have not defiled their garments; and they shall walk with Me in white, for they are worthy." ' "

What Revelation 3:1–4 Means

Sardis, "the dead church," was once the capital of Lydia, a wealthy empire of Asia Minor. Located about thirty miles southeast of Thyatira, Sardis had many citizens who worshiped Caesar and Artemis, the goddess of fertility. Sardis was upscale compared to surrounding cities, with a thriving arts-and-crafts industry. In AD 17, a horrific earthquake devastated the city.

The "seven Spirits" of verse 1 are the sevenfold, fully actualized, complete operational unit of the Holy Spirit, Jesus Christ, and the Father. They are unified and all-powerful. This can be deduced from later verses, such as Revelation 4:5, "Seven lamps of fire were burning before the throne, which are the seven Spirits of God" and Revelation 5:6, "And I looked, and behold, in the midst of the throne and of the four living creatures, and in the midst of the elders, stood a Lamb as though it had been slain, having seven horns and seven eyes, which are the seven Spirits of God sent out into all the earth."

In the Old Testament, Isaiah 11:2 lists seven Spirits, the first being the Spirit of the Lord: "The Spirit of the LORD shall rest upon Him, the Spirit of wisdom and understanding, the Spirit of counsel and might, the Spirit of knowledge and of the fear of the LORD."

Jesus calls the church of Sardis "dead." This signifies that they are basically going through the motions with little-to-no practicing faith.

Jesus' warning that He will come unexpectedly, "as a thief," is mirrored in earlier verses in Scripture. Matthew 24:36 declares, "But of that day and hour no one knows, not even the angels of heaven, but My Father only." Matthew 25:13 states, "Watch therefore, for you know neither the day nor the hour in which the Son of Man is coming."

Revelation 3:1–4 Quiz Answers
1. Jesus said that the church in Sardis is C) dead.
2. Jesus told the church to hold fast and B) repent.
3. The church in Sardis was told that they have but a few names who have not defiled their B) garments.

📖 REVELATION 3:5–8

Pre-Quiz
1. Who would have his name confessed before the Father and His angels?
    A. he who hears
    B. he who overcomes
    C. he who repents

2. Who was told, "I have set before you an open door, and no one can shut it"?
    A. the remaining people of earth
    B. the church of Philadelphia
    C. John

3. The church of Philadelphia was commended by Jesus because they kept His word, and did not deny His
    A. works
    B. deity
    C. name

What the Scriptures Say (Revelation 3:5–8)

"'He who overcomes shall be clothed in white garments, and I will not blot out his name from the Book of Life; but I will confess his name before My Father and before His angels. He who has an ear, let him hear what the Spirit says to the churches.' And to the angel of the church in Philadelphia write, 'These things says He who is holy, He who is true, "He who has the key of David, He who opens and no one shuts, and shuts and no one opens": "I know your works. See, I have set before you an open door, and no one can shut it; for you have a little strength, have kept My word, and have not denied My name."'"

What Revelation 3:5–8 Means

While sinners will be blotted out from the Book of Life, faithful believers will be redeemed forever. White clothing symbolizes that God has watched and recognized godly, obedient, and faithful service. In fact, later in the book of Revelation, we learn that the redeemed of the Lord will wear white in His presence.

Other examples of the color white in Revelation:

   1:14 Jesus' head was white as snow.
   2:17 "I will give him a white stone, and on the stone a new name written."
    3:4 "They shall walk with Me in white."
    3:5 He who overcomes will be dressed in white.
   3:18 Heaven's citizens will be clothed in white.
    4:4 The twenty-four elders were dressed in white.
   6:11 The martyrs wore white robes.
    7:9 Multitudes of the redeemed were dressed in white robes.
   7:14 Robes were made white in the blood of the Lamb.
  19:11 The Lord will come on a white horse.
  19:14 His armies, dressed in white, will be on white horses.

Philadelphia was a relatively small city about forty miles southeast of Sardis. It was founded by Attalus II Philadelphus (ruled 159–138 BC). Its location was ripe for wine production, which was its chief industry.

The church in Philadelphia was a faithful, humble church. It was exceptional in its worship and dedication to Christ, because it was situated in a corrupt, pagan environment. *Philadelphia* means "brotherly love." Jesus loved the church in Philadelphia. In His letter, He offers no criticism of the church.

In verse 7, "He who has the key of David" represents Jesus, the One who has the power and authority to open and shut doors in the Davidic kingdom. Isaiah 22:22 reads, "The key of the house of David I will lay on his shoulder; so he shall open, and no one shall shut; and he shall shut, and no one shall open."

Jesus acknowledges that the church in Philadelphia has "little strength," referring to its small membership in relation to the other six churches.

Revelation 3:5–8 Quiz Answers
1. Who would have his name confessed before the Father and His angels? B) he who overcomes
2. Who was told, "I have set before you an open door, and no one can shut it"? B) the church of Philadelphia
3. The church of Philadelphia was commended by Jesus because they kept His word, and did not deny His C) name.

📖 REVELATION 3:9–12

Pre-Quiz
1. Because the church in Philadelphia kept Jesus' command to persevere, He promised to keep them from the hour of
   A. torment
   B. trial
   C. devastation

2. Because Jesus is coming quickly, the church was told to hold fast so that no one could take their
   A. crown
   B. congregation
   C. glory

3. What did Jesus say would come down out of heaven from My God?
   A. an army of angels
   B. the New Jerusalem
   C. the sun, moon, and stars

What the Scriptures Say (Revelation 3:9–12)

"Indeed I will make those of the synagogue of Satan, who say they are Jews and are not, but lie—indeed I will make them come and worship before your feet, and to know that I have loved you. Because you have kept My command to persevere, I also will keep you from the hour of trial which shall come upon the whole world, to test those who dwell on the earth. Behold, I am coming quickly! Hold fast what you have, that no one may take your crown. He who overcomes, I will make him a pillar in the temple of My God, and he shall go out no more. I will write on him the name of My God and the name of the city of My God, the New Jerusalem, which comes down out of heaven from My God. And I will write on him My new name."

What Revelation 3:9–12 Means

Some people in Philadelphia claimed to be Jews, but actually were of Satan. They would ultimately be forced to come to the church and worship, acknowledging that Christ loves His followers.

Jesus promises the church in Philadelphia that He will keep them from the "hour of trial." This is the catastrophic judgment of the "time of trouble" prophesied in Daniel 12:1: "At that time Michael shall stand up, the great prince who stands watch over the sons of your people; and there shall be a time of trouble, such as never was since there was a nation, even to that time. And at that time your people shall be delivered, every one who is found written in the book," as well as the "great tribulation" prophesized in Matthew 24:21: "For then there will be great tribulation, such as has not been since the beginning of the world until this time, no, nor ever shall be."

Jesus assures the church in Philadelphia that He will either protect them during the period of devastating tribulation, or remove them before the Tribulation. In either case, they will not be involved in this period of suffering and havoc.

On several occasions Jesus warns of an amazing quickness to His return. It is a warning to everyone to be prepared and ready, in a continual state of faithfulness, because His return will be sudden and without warning.

The "pillar" in verse 12 symbolizes stability and strength, such as a pillar of a well-constructed building. Anyone who is a "pillar in the temple" will have a position in Christ's kingdom.

The "new name" in verse 12 refers to receiving the name of God. Just as Satan's followers will receive the "mark of the beast," God's people will be given a "new name," symbolic of citizenship with God. This does not refer to an actual name change, as from Michael to Charles, but a symbolic name, such as "citizen of God" or "belonging to God."

Revelation 3:9–12 Quiz Answers

1. Because the church in Philadelphia kept Jesus' command to persevere, He promised to keep them from the hour of B) trial.
2. Because Jesus is coming quickly, the church was told to hold fast so that no one could take their A) crown.
3. What did Jesus say would come down out of heaven from My God? B) the New Jerusalem

📖 REVELATION 3:13–18

Pre-Quiz

1. Because the church of Laodiceans was neither cold nor hot, Jesus scolded them, saying He would
   A. destroy the church
   B. vomit them out of His mouth
   C. forbid them entry into heaven

2. Because the church of Laodiceans was rich and felt they had need of nothing, not even God, they were called
   A. wretched, miserable, poor, blind, and naked
   B. self-sustaining but ignorant
   C. lacking, deficient, immoral, unworthy, and poor

3. What did Jesus counsel the church of Laodiceans to buy from Him?
   A. a way into heaven
   B. gold refined in the fire
   C. repentance

What the Scriptures Say (Revelation 3:13–18)

"He who has an ear, let him hear what the Spirit says to the churches." And to the angel of the church of the Laodiceans write, "These things says the Amen, the Faithful and True Witness, the Beginning of the creation of God: 'I know your works, that you are neither cold nor hot. I could wish you were cold or hot. So then, because you are lukewarm, and neither cold nor hot, I will vomit you out of My mouth. Because you say, "I am rich, have become wealthy, and have need of nothing"—and do not know that you are wretched, miserable, poor, blind, and naked—I counsel you to buy from Me gold refined in the fire, that you may be rich; and white garments, that you may be clothed, that the shame of your nakedness may not be revealed; and anoint your eyes with eye salve, that you may see.' "

What Revelation 3:13–18 Means

Laodicea, whose name means "justice of the people," was a wealthy city with its own medical school, textile industry, and robust banking system. It was founded by Antichus II (ruled 261–246 BC) and was situated along one of Asia's major trade routes. It is believed that Cicero cashed bank drafts there in 51 BC.

The city manufactured an extremely popular eye salve called collyrium, and the city's water supply came from the city of Hierapolis, an ancient Greek city that rested on hot springs. Coincidentally or not, the water arrived in Laodicea neither hot nor cold, but lukewarm.

"He who has an ear" is in contrast to those who refuse to hear the Lord and want nothing to do with Him. Those who don't hear are chastised in Acts 28:27: "For the hearts of this people have grown dull. Their ears are hard of hearing, and their eyes they have closed, lest they should see with their eyes and hear with their ears, lest they should understand with their hearts and turn, so that I should heal them."

Vividly, Jesus shows His disdain for half-hearted worship in verse 16: "So then, because you are lukewarm, and neither cold nor hot, I will vomit you out of My mouth." The church of Laodicea was wealthy, self-satisfied, and smug. But despite its material wealth, it was needy and impoverished spiritually.

"And anoint your eyes with eye salve, that you may see" is a direct reference from Jesus that personalizes the letter since Laodicea was a major producer of eye salve. This bit of word play would have a powerful impact on the church.

Revelation 3:13–18 Quiz Answers

1. Because the church of Laodiceans was neither cold nor hot, Jesus scolded them, saying He would B) vomit them out of His mouth.
2. Because the church of Laodiceans was rich and felt they had need of nothing, not even God, they were called A) wretched, miserable, poor, blind, and naked.
3. What did Jesus counsel the church of Laodiceans to buy from Him? B) gold refined in the fire

📖 REVELATION 3:19–22

Pre-Quiz

    1. Complete this line: "As many as I love, I rebuke and _____."
       A. love
       B. chasten
       C. punish

    2. Jesus stands at the door and knocks. To those who open the door
       He will come in to them and
       A. dine with them
       B. live with them
       C. pray with them

    3. He who has an ear, let him hear what the Spirit says to
       A. the soul
       B. the churches
       C. the inner man

What the Scriptures Say (Revelation 3:19–22)

"As many as I love, I rebuke and chasten. Therefore be zealous and repent. Behold, I stand at the door and knock. If anyone hears My voice and opens the door, I will come in to him and dine with him, and he with Me. To him who overcomes I will grant to sit with Me on My throne, as I also overcame and sat down with My Father on His throne."

"He who has an ear, let him hear what the Spirit says to the churches."

What Revelation 3:19–22 Means

    As Creator, the Lord can punish and rebuke. The first example of this is Adam and Eve disobeying God's command to not eat from the tree of the knowledge of good and evil. But God's rebuke is an act of love, as we are to gain from rebuke.

Hebrews 12:10 states, "For they indeed for a few days chastened us as seemed best to them, but He for our profit, that we may be partakers of His holiness." This implies that God chastises us so we may be partakers of His holiness, not as random acts of retribution or vengeance. Again, Jesus calls for repentance.

For Jesus to "stand at the door and knock" of His own church is an indictment of the church and signifies that a church can operate as a church of Christ with little-to-no evidence of Christ within the church. It is acceptable to view this verse in another way, in which Jesus stands at the entrance to an unbeliever's heart, ready to come in and make His life-changing presence manifest.

As in all the letters, Jesus has a special invitation and victory for "him who overcomes."

Revelation 3:19–22 Quiz Answers

1. Complete this line: "As many as I love, I rebuke and _____." B) chasten
2. Jesus stands at the door and knocks. To those who open the door He will come in to them and A) dine with them.
3. He who has an ear, let him hear what the Spirit says to B) the churches.

QUICK FACT: Of the seven church cities, the two good ones, Philadelphia and Smyrna, now the modern-day Alasehir and Izmir in Turkey, continue to thrive. The two bad church cities, Sardis and Laodicea, are now desolate, uninhabited locations.

The seven churches are representative of all churches of the time, and churches now.

Breakdown of the Seven Churches

	Praise	Criticism	Command	Promise
Ephesus (2:1–7)	Rejects sin and evil, stays fast in the Lord	No longer enthusiastic for Christ	Return to the works you once did	The tree of life
Smyrna (2:8–11)	Faithfully copes through trials	No criticism	Be faithful until death	The crown of life
Pergamos (2:12–17)	Is faithful	Allows immorality, false doctrines, and idolatry	Repent	Hidden manna, a stone with a new name
Thyatira (2:18–29)	Love, patience, faithful service	Allows cult activity, idolatry, and immorality	Judgment forth-coming, keep the faith	Rules over the nations, the morning star
Sardis (3:1–6)	Some have been faithful	The church is dead	Repent, empower, and strengthen what's left	The faithful will be honored and clothed in white
Philadelphia (3:7–13)	Is faithful, keeps the word of Christ, and honors Him	No criticism	Continue to be faithful	A place in the presence of God, a new name, and the New Jerusalem
Laodicea (3:14–22)	None, no praise at all	Apathy and indifference	Repent and be zealous	Share the throne of Christ

REVELATION

HEAVENLY JOHN

Chapter 4 of Revelation marks a dramatic shift from the previous three chapters and begins the prophecies of horrific future events.

📖 Revelation 4:1–4

Pre-Quiz

1. The first voice that John heard was like that of a
   A. raven
   B. trumpet
   C. angel

2. What did John see around the throne?
   A. a rainbow
   B. doves
   C. fiery stars

3. Around the throne were how many additional thrones?
   A. three
   B. seven
   C. twenty-four

What the Scriptures Say (Revelation 4:1)

"After these things I looked, and behold, a door standing open in heaven. And the first voice which I heard was like a trumpet speaking with me, saying, 'Come up here, and I will show you things which must take place after this.'"

What Revelation 4:1 Means

John enters heaven after hearing the trumpet voice instruct him to "Come up." This is symbolic and representative of the rapture of the church when the sounding of the trumpet will herald the dead in Christ to rise and be resurrected. At this time, the faithful who are still alive will be transformed and both groups will be raptured in the air to meet Christ.

This is supported by 1 Corinthians 15:20–21: "But now Christ is risen from the dead, and has become the firstfruits of those who have fallen asleep. For since by man came death, by Man also came the resurrection of the dead."

What the Scriptures Say (Revelation 4:2)

Immediately I was in the Spirit; and behold, a throne set in heaven, and One sat on the throne.

What Revelation 4:2 Means

John becoming "immediately" in the Spirit is reminiscent of how quickly Jesus will come.

What the Scriptures Say (Revelation 4:3–4)

And He who sat there was like a jasper and a sardius stone in appearance; and there was a rainbow around the throne, in appearance like an emerald. Around the throne were twenty-four thrones, and on the thrones I saw twenty-four elders sitting, clothed in white robes; and they had crowns of gold on their heads.

What Revelation 4:3–4 Means

The throne of God is the dominant feature of heaven, as everything revolves around it. John uses brilliant gems, a jasper stone, and a sardius to describe God.

The rainbow around the throne is a reminder of God's covenant with mankind in which He promises to never destroy the earth by flood, as stated in Genesis 9:12–13: "And God said: 'This is the sign of the covenant which I make between Me and you, and every living creature that is with you, for perpetual generations: I set My rainbow in the cloud, and it shall be for the sign of the covenant between Me and the earth.'"

Revelation 4:1–4 Quiz Answers

1. The first voice that John heard was like that of a B) trumpet.
2. What did John see around the throne? A) a rainbow
3. Around the throne were how many additional thrones? C) twenty-four

📖 REVELATION 4:5–7

Pre-Quiz

1. Before the throne was a sea of
   A. gold
   B. glass
   C. blood

2. The first living creature John saw was a
   A. man
   B. eagle
   C. lion

3. How many living creatures did John see around the throne?

   A. two

   B. four

   C. seven

What the Scriptures Say (Revelation 4:5–7)

And from the throne proceeded lightnings, thunderings, and voices. Seven lamps of fire were burning before the throne, which are the seven Spirits of God. Before the throne there was a sea of glass, like crystal. And in the midst of the throne, and around the throne, were four living creatures full of eyes in front and in back. The first living creature was like a lion, the second living creature like a calf, the third living creature had a face like a man, and the fourth living creature was like a flying eagle.

What Revelation 4:5–7 Means

This passage of Scripture gives us a small glimpse into the majesty of heaven. The "sea of glass" signifies a calmness and serenity. An agitated sea rumbles and roars, yet this heavenly description brings to mind a sea so still and calm that it is smooth as glass.

The four living creatures are angels, specifically seraphim. Isaiah first describes them in Isaiah 6:1–3:

In the year that King Uzziah died, I saw the Lord sitting on a throne, high and lifted up, and the train of His robe filled the temple. Above it stood seraphim; each one had six wings: with two he covered his face, with two he covered his feet, and with two he flew. And one cried to another and said:

"Holy, holy, holy is the Lord of hosts;

The whole earth is full of His glory!"

Revelation 4:5–7 Quiz Answers

1. Before the throne was a sea of B) glass.

2. The first living creature John saw was a C) lion.

3. How many living creatures did John see around the throne? B) four

📖 REVELATION 4:8–11

Pre-Quiz

1. How many elders fall down before Him?
   A. eleven
   B. twenty-four
   C. forty-eight

2. What do the elders cast before the throne?
   A. gold coins
   B. burning incense
   C. their crowns

3. The elders call the Lord
   A. worthy
   B. gracious
   C. awesome

What the Scriptures Say (Revelation 4:8–11)

The four living creatures, each having six wings, were full of eyes around and within. And they do not rest day or night, saying:

> "Holy, holy, holy,
> Lord God Almighty,
> Who was and is and is to come!"

Whenever the living creatures give glory and honor and thanks to Him who sits on the throne, who lives forever and ever, the twenty-four elders fall down before Him who sits on the throne and worship Him who lives forever and ever, and cast their crowns before the throne, saying:

> "You are worthy, O Lord,
> To receive glory and honor and power;

    For You created all things,

    And by Your will they exist and were created."

What Revelation 4:8–11 Means

These verses are verses of confirmation. The four living creatures confirm that Christ "is to come."

The twenty-four elders confirm that God the Creator made humans for His enjoyment and pleasure.

Revelation 4:8–11 Quiz Answers

1. How many elders fall down before Him? B) twenty-four
2. What do the elders cast before the throne? C) their crowns
3. The elders call the Lord A) worthy.

REVELATION

5

JESUS ON THE THRONE

📖 REVELATION 5:1–4

Pre-Quiz

1. What was in the right hand of Him who sat on the throne?
   A. a lightning bolt
   B. a scroll
   C. the book of life

2. Who wanted to know who is worthy to open the scroll and loose its seals?
   A. John
   B. a strong angel
   C. God

3. What did John do because no one was able to open the scroll?
   A. He volunteered.
   B. He fainted.
   C. He wept.

What the Scriptures Say (Revelation 5:1–4)

And I saw in the right hand of Him who sat on the throne a scroll written inside and on the back, sealed with seven seals. Then I saw a strong angel proclaiming with a loud voice, "Who is worthy to open the scroll and to loose its seals?" And no one in heaven or on the earth or under the earth was able to open the scroll, or to look at it. So I wept much, because no one was found worthy to open and read the scroll, or to look at it.

What Revelation 5:1–4 Means

The "scroll," or book, is in the right hand of God the Father. The "right hand" indicates power. What John sees is not a printed book as one would read today because there were no printed books at that time in history.

John sees a scroll, a manuscript with writing on both sides, and rolled to form a scroll secured or "sealed" with seven seals. It is possible that the scroll was made up of seven individual parchments rolled up together, with each parchment secured to make it necessary to break one of the seven seals to get to the next parchment.

The "strong angel" who inquires about who is worthy to open the scroll and loosen the seals is most likely Michael, since the descriptor of the angel is "strong." Although the strong angel asks the question, the answer is obvious in that only God is able to open the seals, again an indication of God's power and strength.

John weeps because no one was found who was worthy to open the seals.

Revelation 5:1–4 Quiz Answers

1. What was in the right hand of Him who sat on the throne? B) a scroll
2. Who wanted to know who is worthy to open the scroll and loose its seals? B) a strong angel
3. What did John do because no one was able to open the scroll? C) He wept.

📖 REVELATION 5:5–8

Pre-Quiz

1. Who prevailed to open the scroll and loose the seven seals?
   A. John
   B. the archangel
   C. Jesus

2. What stood in the midst of the elders appearing as though it had been slain?
   A. a ram
   B. a dove
   C. a lamb

3. What musical instrument did each of the twenty-four elders have?
   A. a harp
   B. a trumpet
   C. a timpani

What the Scriptures Say (Revelation 5:5–8)

But one of the elders said to me, "Do not weep. Behold, the Lion of the tribe of Judah, the Root of David, has prevailed to open the scroll and to loose its seven seals." And I looked, and behold, in the midst of the throne and of the four living creatures, and in the midst of the elders, stood a Lamb as though it had been slain, having seven horns and seven eyes, which are the seven Spirits of God sent out into all the earth. Then He came and took the scroll out of the right hand of Him who sat on the throne. Now when He had taken the scroll, the four living creatures and the twenty-four elders fell down before the Lamb, each having a harp, and golden bowls full of incense, which are the prayers of the saints.

What Revelation 5:5–8 Means

One of the twenty-four elders instructs John not to weep, because the Lion of the tribe of Judah is worthy to loosen the seals. The Lion of Judah and the Root of David are titles for Jesus Christ. Jesus has "prevailed" to loose the seals by virtue of His victory over Satan.

The "Lamb as though it had been slain" refers to Jesus Christ whom John the Baptist recognized in John 1:29: "The next day John saw Jesus coming toward him, and said, 'Behold! The Lamb of God who takes away the sin of the world!' "

Horns represent power and the authority to rule. This is confirmed in Daniel 7:24: "The ten horns are ten kings who shall arise from this kingdom. And another shall rise after them; He shall be different from the first ones, and shall subdue three kings."

This is the first direct reference from John that Jesus is in heaven. Jesus was not sitting, rather He "stood." Jesus took the scroll out of the right hand of Him who sits on the throne, the Father, and now Jesus has been given authority over the judgment of the earth. This mirrors Daniel 7:13–14: "I was watching in the night visions, and behold, One like the Son of Man, coming with the clouds of heaven! He came to the Ancient of Days, and they brought Him near before Him. Then to Him was given dominion and glory and a kingdom, that all peoples, nations, and languages should serve Him. His dominion is an everlasting dominion, which shall not pass away, and His kingdom the one which shall not be destroyed."

Revelation 5:5–8 Quiz Answers

1. Who prevailed to open the scroll and loose the seven seals? C) Jesus
2. What stood in the midst of the elders appearing as though it had been slain? C) a lamb
3. What musical instrument did each of the twenty-four elders have? A) a harp

📖 REVELATION 5:9–14

Pre-Quiz

1. According to Revelation 5:9, we are redeemed to God by Jesus'
   A. prayers
   B. power
   C. blood

2. Around the throne, John heard the voices of many
   A. people mourning and wailing
   B. angels
   C. people celebrating

3. Now John heard the voice of many angels, living creatures, and elders that he numbered as
   A. multitudes upon multitudes
   B. ten thousand times ten thousand, and thousands of thousands
   C. millions upon millions upon millions

What the Scriptures Say (Revelation 5:9–14)

And they sang a new song, saying:

> "You are worthy to take the scroll,
> And to open its seals;
> For You were slain,
> And have redeemed us to God by Your blood
> Out of every tribe and tongue and people and nation,
> And have made us kings and priests to our God;
> And we shall reign on the earth."

Then I looked, and I heard the voice of many angels around the throne, the living creatures, and the elders; and the number of them was ten thousand times ten thousand, and thousands of thousands, saying with a loud voice:

"Worthy is the Lamb who was slain
To receive power and riches and wisdom,
And strength and honor and glory and blessing!"

And every creature which is in heaven and on the earth and under the earth and such as are in the sea, and all that are in them, I heard saying:

"Blessing and honor and glory and power
Be to Him who sits on the throne,
And to the Lamb, forever and ever!"

Then the four living creatures said, "Amen!" And the twenty-four elders fell down and worshiped Him who lives forever and ever.

What Revelation 5:9–14 Means

The song that they sang to Jesus has very telling lyrics. God's people are most assuredly in heaven. In fact, there is no mention of the churches being on earth in the book of Revelation after the third chapter. The saints have been redeemed, caught up in the air, and are in heaven. No saints of God will go through the Tribulation.

The lyrics sung are a testimony to Christ from His redeemed. In heaven, "And have redeemed us to God by Your blood" can only refer to Jesus and the people of the earth whom He has redeemed, who are now in heaven with Him.

John saw an innumerable amount of angels around the throne.

Revelation 5:9–14 Quiz Answers

1. According to Revelation 5:9, we are redeemed to God by Jesus' C) blood.
2. Around the throne, John heard the voices of many B) angels.

3. Now John heard the voice of many angels, living creatures, and elders that he numbered as B) ten thousand times ten thousand, and thousands of thousands.

The Lamb

In the book of Revelation, Jesus is called "the Lamb" more than any other name.

- The Lamb took the sealed scroll (book) and opened it (5:6–7; 6:1).
- The elders and the living creatures worship the Lamb (5:8,14).
- Ten thousand times ten thousand and thousands and thousands of angels worship the Lamb (5:11–13).
- The day of the Lamb's wrath is come (6:16–17).
- Multitudes from all the nations worship the Lamb (7:9–10).
- Their robes were washed in the blood of the Lamb (7:14).
- The Lamb leads them to fountains of living waters (7:17).
- They overcame Satan by the blood of the Lamb (12:11).
- The 144,000 follow the Lamb (14:1, 4).
- They sing the song of Moses and the Lamb (15:3).
- The Lamb is Lord of lords and King of kings (17:14).
- The marriage of the Lamb to His bride has come (19:7, 9; 21:9).
- The twelve foundations of the city are named for the twelve apostles of the Lamb (21:14).
- The Lamb is the temple and the light of the city (21:22, 23).
- Only those in the Lamb's Book of Life shall enter (21:27).
- Water of life flows from the throne of the Lamb (22:1, 3).

REVELATION

6

THE LAMB AND THE SCROLLS

📖 REVELATION 6:1–8

Pre-Quiz

1. What creature was spotted upon the opening of the first seal?
   A. a white bear
   B. a white horse
   C. a white lion

2. What color is associated with the creature mentioned in the opening of the second seal?
   A. blue
   B. red
   C. black

3. When the fourth seal was opened, who sat on the pale horse?
   A. the angel of grief
   B. the avenger
   C. Death

What the Scriptures Say (Revelation 6:1)

Now I saw when the Lamb opened one of the seals; and I heard one of the four living creatures saying with a voice like thunder, "Come and see."

What Revelation 6:1 Means

Now we enter the section of Revelation that deals with the opening of the seals by the Lamb (Jesus) who was found worthy to open them. We begin to learn of the events that will take place on earth during the seven years of Tribulation. The opening of the seals follows a specific sequence that is in the exact order as Jesus reveals in Matthew 24.

What the Scriptures Say (Revelation 6:2)

And I looked, and behold, a white horse. He who sat on it had a bow; and a crown was given to him, and he went out conquering and to conquer.

What Revelation 6:2 Means

The rider on the white horse is not Jesus. It is the Antichrist. The bow indicates he is a warrior, but it is telling that he has no arrow, indicating that he will use diplomacy to take over control of this war-weary world. A world that is so tired of wars and rumors of war that they will trade national sovereignty and personal freedom for the offer of "peace" if they will let him be the leader of the world. As we will see in chapter 6, his ruse is impossible as three countries rebel and the world is plunged into the next world war.

We can be assured that despite the rider having a white horse, he is indeed the Antichrist and not Jesus, who carries a two-edged sword throughout Scripture. Isn't the fact that the rider of the white horse has a bow but no arrow indicative of an enemy who is not all-powerful? A bow with no arrow is indicative of a pseudo-warrior. Also, Jesus has several crowns and would not need to be given one.

So now we have, with the opening of the first seal, the Antichrist heading to earth and the onset of the seven-year Tribulation.

For decades, many have taught that we were currently in the Tribulation period already, which is contradictory to what Scripture says about the

Tribulation period being only seven years. How can one teach for fifteen years, for example, that we are in the seven-year-long Tribulation period?

Who is the Antichrist? The Antichrist is not Satan. They are two different beings, with Satan being the stronger of the two. Second Thessalonians 2:9 reveals that the Antichrist gets his power and authority from Satan: "The coming of the lawless one is according to the working of Satan, with all power, signs, and lying wonders."

Second Thessalonians 2:3 states, "Let no one deceive you by any means; for that Day will not come unless the falling away comes first, and the man of sin is revealed, the son of perdition." (Perdition means damnation or spiritual ruin.) Verse 6 continues, "And now you know what is restraining, that he may be revealed in his own time." Here the Antichrist is described as a man of sin and the son of perdition.

What the Scriptures Say (Revelation 6:3–4)

When He opened the second seal, I heard the second living creature saying, "Come and see." Another horse, fiery red, went out. And it was granted to the one who sat on it to take peace from the earth, and that people should kill one another; and there was given to him a great sword.

What Revelation 6:3–4 Means

The opening of the second seal unleashes the rider on the red horse who, armed with a great sword, is empowered to remove peace from the earth. Wars occur upon the earth, and this verse is remindful of the prophecy of Matthew 24:7–8: "For nation will rise against nation, and kingdom against kingdom. And there will be famines, pestilences, and earthquakes in various places. All these are the beginning of sorrows."

But what "peace" will be on earth? What peace is there to remove? This could possibly be the false peace that results for a short time after the Antichrist signs a covenant with Israel for seven years (Dan. 9:27), that Daniel was later told he would break his word and plunge Israel into the worst holocaust against Israel in history. This is all described, as we shall see later, in the book of Revelation.

The exact timing of this event is not agreed upon, though there is no question that it will be soon, for the players in the scene are the exact neighbors of Israel today and have a unanimous hatred for God's chosen people. Some prophecy scholars think this will occur shortly before the Rapture; others think it will be shortly after. The thing to remember is, it could be very soon.

While no one can know "the day or the hour" of the Rapture, it cannot be denied that we are in or near "the season" of the time these events will take place.

The most detailed description of this war that the Antichrist will have to put down at great loss of life is one of the most astounding prophecies in the Bible, described in Ezekiel 38–39.

Ezekiel 38:12 paints a future Israel as a land of plenty: "to take plunder and to take booty, to stretch out your hand against the waste places that are again inhabited, and against a people gathered from the nations, who have acquired livestock and goods, who dwell in the midst of the land."

A few verses earlier, Ezekiel 38:2–8 reveals that Russia and its Middle Eastern allies will try to overtake the plentiful Israel and strip and plunder it of its resources. Gog and Magog is Russia; Persia is Iran.

Son of man, set your face against Gog, of the land of Magog, the prince of Rosh, Meshech, and Tubal, and prophesy against him, and say, "Thus says the Lord God: Behold, I am against you, O Gog, the prince of Rosh, Meshech, and Tubal. I will turn you around, put hooks into your jaws, and lead you out, with all your army, horses, and horsemen, all splendidly clothed, a great company with bucklers and shields, all of them handling swords. Persia, Ethiopia, and Libya are with them, all of them with shield and helmet; Gomer and all its troops; the house of Togarmah from the far north and all its troops—many people are with you.

"Prepare yourself and be ready, you and all your companies that are gathered about you; and be a guard for them. After many days you will be visited. In the latter years you will come into the land of those brought back from the sword and gathered from many people on the mountains of Israel, which had long been desolate; they were brought out of the nations, and now all of them dwell safely."

This brief time of peace should not be confused with the one-thousand-year period of peace at the end of the Tribulation, in which the entire world will reside in peace.

In verse 4, red represents bloodshed. The result from the second seal is not the Battle of Armageddon, but the next world war, which begins right after the rapture of God's people. This is a very brief war, lasting only about twenty-four hours. Ezekiel 38–39 outlines this war.

What the Scriptures Say (Revelation 6:5–6)

When He opened the third seal, I heard the third living creature say, "Come and see." So I looked, and behold, a black horse, and he who sat on it had a pair of scales in his hand. And I heard a voice in the midst of the four living creatures saying, "A quart of wheat for a denarius, and three quarts of barley for a denarius; and do not harm the oil and the wine."

What Revelation 6:5–6 Means

A black horse is released upon the opening of the third seal. The rider of the black horse has a pair of scales. This represents famine. The scales are used to measure grain by weight. The extremely high costs of grain in these passages are representative of about one-eighth of what could normally be bought for the same amount of money, a valuable silver coin called the denarius, which was typical pay for one day's work. This alludes to the "famines" portion of Matthew 24:7–8.

The command to "not harm the oil and the wine" alludes to limits God placed on the famine; it cannot be completely devastating. The oil is olive oil extracted from the fruit of the olive tree, and wine is from fruit of the vine, both of which have strong, deep roots that may not be immediately affected by famine conditions. This will not be a worldwide famine, but will be devastating to many regions. This famine involves various food shortages, but not a complete lack of it.

What the Scriptures Say (Revelation 6:7–8)

When He opened the fourth seal, I heard the voice of the fourth living creature saying, "Come and see." So I looked, and behold, a pale horse. And the name of him who sat on it was Death, and Hades followed with him. And power was given to them over a fourth of the earth, to kill with sword, with hunger, with death, and by the beasts of the earth.

What Revelation 6:7–8 Means

The opening of the fourth seal releases a pale horse. Pale, a lack of color, symbolizes the appearance of corpses, and thusly the rider is aptly named Death. Death follows as the natural result of the previous plagues in the land, war, and famine. God brought the nation of Israel to a state of repentance using these same methods: "When there is famine in the land, pestilence or blight or mildew, locusts or grasshoppers; when their enemy besieges them in the land of their cities; whatever plague or whatever sickness there is; whatever prayer, whatever supplication is made by anyone, or by all Your people Israel, when each one knows the plague of his own heart, and spreads out his hands toward this temple" (1 Kings 8:37–38).

Verse 8 has a very important message. Hades follows death. This means that death kills the fleshly body but there is indeed an afterlife, in this case, the soul going to Hades, or a hellish place. Just as the believer's fleshly body can die and the soul goes to heaven, here is a clear indication that the opposite is true for unbelievers. Later in Revelation 20:14–15, it is revealed that the unbeliever will be cast into the lake of fire.

It is important to note that the four horsemen were given power over only one-fourth of the earth, not the entire earth. This seems to contradict teachings of the Antichrist singularly ruling the entire world as head of a one-world government. In fact, this verse clearly shows that God is still in control during this dreadful period of upcoming history, limiting the power and authority of the Antichrist and his forces. Still, there will be much carnage and devastation.

Death will come to one-fourth of the earth's population during a seven-year period. Of about seven billion people on earth today, 1.75 billion would be slain according to verse 8.

QUICK FACT: The four horsemen released with the opening of the first four scrolls is where we obtained the phrase "the four horsemen of the apocalypse."

Revelation 6:1–8 Quiz Answers

1. What creature was spotted upon the opening of the first seal? B) a white horse
2. What color is associated with the creature mentioned in the opening of the second seal? B) red
3. When the fourth seal was opened, who sat on the pale horse? C) Death

📖 REVELATION 6:9–12

Pre-Quiz

1. When Jesus opened the fifth seal, John saw the souls of those who had been slain for
   A. their greed
   B. the Word of God
   C. the sins of the world

2. What was given to each of the souls?
   A. the crown
   B. a white robe
   C. a chance to repent

3. What event occurred upon the opening of the sixth seal?
   A. A volcano erupted.
   B. A great flood overtook the earth.
   C. There was a great earthquake.

What the Scriptures Say (Revelation 6:9–12)

When He opened the fifth seal, I saw under the altar the souls of those who had been slain for the word of God and for the testimony which they held. And they cried with a loud voice, saying, "How long, O Lord, holy and true, until You judge and avenge our blood on those who dwell on the earth?" Then a white robe was given to each of them; and it was said to them that they should rest a little while longer, until both the number of their fellow servants and their brethren, who would be killed as they were, was completed. I looked when He opened the sixth seal, and behold, there was a great earthquake; and the sun became black as sackcloth of hair, and the moon became like blood.

What Revelation 6:9–12 Means

The opening of the fifth seal shifts us from the activities on the earth to the activities in heaven. John sees the souls of martyrs who remained steadfast for God and were killed on earth during the Tribulation. Matthew 24:9–12 details this: "Then they will deliver you up to tribulation and kill you, and you will be hated by all nations for My name's sake. And then many will be offended, will betray one another, and will hate one another. Then many false prophets will rise up and deceive many. And because lawlessness will abound, the love of many will grow cold."

The martyrs beg God for vengeance on their killers, and God tells them to be patient while other would-be martyrs enter heaven. This is reasonable since there will be additional martyrs during the second half of the Tribulation, and others caught up alive at mid-Tribulation. These were martyrs who came to Christ after the Rapture and refused to wear the mark of the Beast, which will be explained in later verses.

Verse 12 covers the opening of the sixth seal, which releases horrific events upon the earth, including a massive earthquake.

Revelation 6:9–12 Quiz Answers

1. When Jesus opened the fifth seal, John saw the souls of those who had been slain for B) the Word of God.
2. What was given to each of the souls? B) a white robe

3. What event occurred upon the opening of the sixth seal? C) There was a great earthquake.

📖 REVELATION 6:13–17

Pre-Quiz

1. In Revelation 6:13, what happened to the stars of heaven?
   A. They fell to earth.
   B. They melted.
   C. They exploded and became dust.

2. What cowardly act did the kings of the earth do?
   A. They hid themselves in caves.
   B. They sacrificed women and children.
   C. They retreated to the rear of their armies.

3. What question did the kings of the earth ask during the great day of His wrath?
   A. What has gone wrong?
   B. What must we do to be saved?
   C. Who is able to stand?

What the Scriptures Say (Revelation 6:13–17)

And the stars of heaven fell to the earth, as a fig tree drops its late figs when it is shaken by a mighty wind. Then the sky receded as a scroll when it is rolled up, and every mountain and island was moved out of its place. And the kings of the earth, the great men, the rich men, the commanders, the mighty men, every slave and every free man, hid themselves in the caves and in the rocks of the mountains, and said to the mountains and rocks, "Fall on us and hide us from the face of Him who sits on the throne and from the wrath of the Lamb! For the great day of His wrath has come, and who is able to stand?"

What Revelation 6:13–17 Means

The entire earth is affected. Nature is turned upside-down as the last day of the Tribulation arrives and Jesus returns to set up His kingdom and rule on earth. This is the Lamb's day of wrath as outlined in Matthew 24:29–31:

> Immediately after the tribulation of those days the sun will be darkened, and the moon will not give its light; the stars will fall from heaven, and the powers of the heavens will be shaken. Then the sign of the Son of Man will appear in heaven, and then all the tribes of the earth will mourn, and they will see the Son of Man coming on the clouds of heaven with power and great glory. And He will send His angels with a great sound of a trumpet, and they will gather together His elect from the four winds, from one end of heaven to the other.

Sinful people, earthly shunners of Jesus, are now terrified of Him and His judgment, seeking to hide from His face at all costs. Yet, no one, not one, will be able to escape Him and His reach.

Revelation 6:13–17 Quiz Answers

1. In Revelation 6:13, what happened to the stars of heaven? A) They fell to earth.
2. What cowardly act did the kings of the earth do? A) They hid themselves in caves.
3. What question did the kings of the earth ask during the great day of His wrath? C) Who is able to stand?

REVELATION

144,000

Revelation 7 shifts us away from the earth and back to heaven. The seventh seal is yet to be opened, and will not be opened until Revelation 8.

📖 Revelation 7:1–4

Pre-Quiz

1. What did John see standing at the four corners of the earth?
   A. four dragons
   B. four angels
   C. four swords

2. Where were the servants of God sealed?
   A. in heaven
   B. on their foreheads
   C. on the palms of their hands

3. John heard the number of those who were sealed. What was it?
   A. multitude upon multitude
   B. 1 million
   C. 144,000

What the Scriptures Say (Revelation 7:1–4)

After these things I saw four angels standing at the four corners of the earth, holding the four winds of the earth, that the wind should not blow on the earth, on the sea, or on any tree. Then I saw another angel ascending from the east, having the seal of the living God. And he cried with a loud voice to the four angels to whom it was granted to harm the earth and the sea, saying, "Do not harm the earth, the sea, or the trees till we have sealed the servants of our God on their foreheads." And I heard the number of those who were sealed. One hundred and forty-four thousand of all the tribes of the children of Israel were sealed.

What Revelation 7:1–4 Means

Even during the devastation, God shows mercy by bringing a sudden, but temporary cessation of the havoc. The earth is spherical, so the imagery of the "four corners" of the earth symbolically represents all the earth.

This Tribulation lull allows time for the 12,000 each from the twelve tribes, 144,000 in all, to be sealed on their foreheads with the mark of God.

The seal is the Father's name imprinted on their foreheads. Seals of that time represented ownership. We also know that these 144,000 are Jews—12,000 from each of the twelve tribes.

Revelation 7:1–4 Quiz Answers

1. What did John see standing at the four corners of the earth? B) four angels
2. Where were the servants of God sealed? B) on their foreheads
3. John heard the number of those who were sealed. What was it? C) 144,000

📖 REVELATION 7:5–10

Pre-Quiz

1. How many were sealed from each of the twelve tribes?

   A. one

   B. seven

   C. twelve thousand

2. John saw a great multitude that no one could number, with what in their hands?

   A. stars

   B. palm branches

   C. thunderbolts

3. The great multitude cried out, proclaiming what belonged to God?

   A. salvation

   B. the universe

   C. vengeance

What the Scriptures Say (Revelation 7:5–10)

... of the tribe of Judah twelve thousand were sealed;

of the tribe of Reuben twelve thousand were sealed;

of the tribe of Gad twelve thousand were sealed;

of the tribe of Asher twelve thousand were sealed;

of the tribe of Naphtali twelve thousand were sealed;

of the tribe of Manasseh twelve thousand were sealed;

of the tribe of Simeon twelve thousand were sealed;

of the tribe of Levi twelve thousand were sealed;

of the tribe of Issachar twelve thousand were sealed;

of the tribe of Zebulun twelve thousand were sealed;

of the tribe of Joseph twelve thousand were sealed;

of the tribe of Benjamin twelve thousand were sealed.

After these things I looked, and behold, a great multitude which no one could number, of all nations, tribes, peoples, and tongues, standing before the throne and before the Lamb, clothed with white robes, with palm branches in their hands, and crying out with a loud voice, saying, "Salvation belongs to our God who sits on the throne, and to the Lamb!"

What Revelation 7:5–10 Means

These are twelve thousand from each of the twelve tribes of Israel. In this list of the twelve tribes of Israel is a major substitution. The tribe of Dan is replaced by Manasseh, one of Joseph's sons.

Revelation 7:5–10 Quiz Answers

1. How many were sealed from each of the twelve tribes? C) twelve thousand
2. John saw a great multitude that no one could number, with what in their hands? B) palm branches
3. The great multitude cried out, proclaiming what belonged to God? A) salvation

📖 REVELATION 7:11–17

Pre-Quiz

1. What question did one of the elders ask concerning those arrayed in white robes?
   A. Where did they come from?
   B. Where are they going?
   C. Who do they worship?

2. What will those before the throne of God do day and night in His temple?
   A. pray
   B. repent
   C. serve Him

3. The Lamb in the midst of the throne will lead them to living
    A. fountains of waters
    B. trees of life
    C. monuments

What the Scriptures Say (Revelation 7:11–17)

All the angels stood around the throne and the elders and the four living creatures, and fell on their faces before the throne and worshiped God, saying:

> "Amen! Blessing and glory and wisdom,
> Thanksgiving and honor and power and might,
> Be to our God forever and ever.
> Amen."

Then one of the elders answered, saying to me, "Who are these arrayed in white robes, and where did they come from?"

And I said to him, "Sir, you know."

So he said to me, "These are the ones who come out of the great tribulation, and washed their robes and made them white in the blood of the Lamb. Therefore they are before the throne of God, and serve Him day and night in His temple. And He who sits on the throne will dwell among them. They shall neither hunger anymore nor thirst anymore; the sun shall not strike them, nor any heat; for the Lamb who is in the midst of the throne will shepherd them and lead them to living fountains of waters. And God will wipe away every tear from their eyes."

What Revelation 7:11–17 Means

A great multitude will come "out of the great tribulation." These are martyrs who repented and accepted Jesus Christ during the Tribulation time of great human loss and devastation. With their robes "made . . . white" by the "blood of the Lamb," these martyrs have been fully accepted by Christ.

Revelation 7:11–17 Quiz Answers

1. What question did one of the elders ask concerning those arrayed in white robes? A) Where did they come from?
2. What will those before the throne of God do day and night in His temple? C) serve Him
3. The Lamb in the midst of the throne will lead them to living A) fountains of waters.

REVELATION

THE SEVENTH SEAL

📖 REVELATION 8:1–3

Pre-Quiz

1. When Jesus opened the seventh seal, what happened in heaven for about half an hour?
   A. There were thunderous storms.
   B. There was silence.
   C. Legions of angels were dispatched.

2. What was given to the seven angels who will stand before God?
   A. seven bows and seven arrows
   B. seven bits of grain
   C. seven trumpets

3. What ascended before God with the smoke of the incense?
   A. the sins of the world
   B. the prayers of the saints
   C. the angels preparing for war

What the Scriptures Say (Revelation 8:1–3)

When He opened the seventh seal, there was silence in heaven for about half an hour. And I saw the seven angels who stand before God, and to them were given seven trumpets. Then another angel, having a golden censer, came and stood at the altar. He was given much incense, that he should offer it with the prayers of all the saints upon the golden altar which was before the throne.

What Revelation 8:1–3 Means

There is no obvious reason to explain the thirty-minute silence after the opening of the seventh seal. It could be an indication that something incredible is about to happen as heaven virtually comes to a halt. Since heaven is described as a joyful place of many sounds, praising, music, and the like, the silence here seems to be a grave precursor to something momentous about to occur.

Revelation 8 begins in the middle of the Tribulation as the opening of the seventh seal starts the trumpet judgments. These judgments of the seventh seal are worse than all six previous judgments, which could explain the ominous thirty-minute silence in heaven that preceded the opening.

An eighth angel comes before God with a golden censer, which has a direct relationship to the prayers of the saints. A censer is a container typically used for burning incense.

Revelation 8:1–3 Quiz Answers

1. When Jesus opened the seventh seal, what happened in heaven for about half an hour? B) There was silence.
2. What was given to the seven angels who will stand before God? C) seven trumpets
3. What ascended before God with the smoke of the incense? B) the prayers of the saints

📖 REVELATION 8:4–8

Pre-Quiz

1. When the angel took the censer, filled it with fire from the altar, and threw it to earth, what occurred?

   A. noises, thunderings, lightnings, and an earthquake

   B. complete silence

   C. pestilence, famine, eruptings, and violence

2. When the first angel sounded its trumpet, hail and fire followed mingled with

   A. salt

   B. blood

   C. vinegar

3. When the second angel sounded its trumpet, what was thrown into the sea?

   A. a great mountain burning with fire

   B. a ram, lamb, and goat

   C. the seven seals

What the Scriptures Say (Revelation 8:4–5)

And the smoke of the incense, with the prayers of the saints, ascended before God from the angel's hand. Then the angel took the censer, filled it with fire from the altar, and threw it to the earth. And there were noises, thunderings, lightnings, and an earthquake.

What Revelation 8:4–5 Means

God recognizes the prayers of the saints from the smoke of the censer. As it is filled with fire and hurled to the earth, the mid-Tribulation disruption of nature begins.

What the Scriptures Say (Revelation 8:6)

So the seven angels who had the seven trumpets prepared themselves
to sound.

What Revelation 8:6 Means

The seven angels who had the seven trumpets are most likely the seven
angels of the churches from Revelation 1:4, which reads, "John, to the seven
churches which are in Asia. Grace to you and peace from Him who is and
who was and who is to come, and from the seven spirits who are before His
throne." Revelation 1:20 is also an apt reference: "The mystery of the seven
stars which you saw in My right hand, and the seven golden lampstands:
The seven stars are the angels of the seven churches, and the seven lampstands which you saw are the seven churches." As previously stated, the
seven spirits mentioned in Revelation 1:4 is the sevenfold ministry of the
Holy Spirit. Isaiah 11:2 reads, "The Spirit of the Lord shall rest upon Him,
the Spirit of wisdom and understanding, the Spirit of counsel and might,
the Spirit of knowledge and of the fear of the Lord."

What the Scriptures Say (Revelation 8:7–8)

The first angel sounded: And hail and fire followed, mingled with blood,
and they were thrown to the earth. And a third of the trees were burned
up, and all green grass was burned up. Then the second angel sounded:
And something like a great mountain burning with fire was thrown into
the sea, and a third of the sea became blood.

What Revelation 8:7–8 Means

In rapid succession, the first two trumpets sound, and severe devastation unfolds. It is clear that the trumpet judgments are more severe
than other judgments. The strange mixture of hail, fire, and blood shows
another supernatural aspect of the judgment. It is important to note that
these catastrophes do not occur instantaneously but over a period of three
and a half years, the final years of the Tribulation.

In verse 8, the term "like a great mountain" indicates the object is not a literal mountain, yet is powerful enough to destroy one-third of all the fish and ships in the sea.

Revelation 8:4–8 Quiz Answers
1. When the angel took the censer, filled it with fire from the altar, and threw it to earth, what occurred? A) noises, thunderings, lightnings, and an earthquake
2. When the first angel sounded its trumpet, hail and fire followed mingled with B) blood.
3. When the second angel sounded its trumpet, what was thrown into the sea? A) a great mountain burning with fire

📖 REVELATION 8:9–11

Pre-Quiz
1. What percentage of ships and living creatures in the sea were destroyed?
   A. one-tenth
   B. one-half
   C. one-third

2. When the third angel sounded its trumpet, what fell from heaven?
   A. a great star
   B. one-third of all the angels
   C. fire and brimstone

3. What is Wormwood?
   A. Satan
   B. a great star that fell from heaven
   C. the head of the warring angels

What the Scriptures Say (Revelation 8:9–11)

And a third of the living creatures in the sea died, and a third of the ships were destroyed. Then the third angel sounded: And a great star fell from heaven, burning like a torch, and it fell on a third of the rivers and on the springs of water. The name of the star is Wormwood. A third of the waters became wormwood, and many men died from the water, because it was made bitter.

What Revelation 8:9–11 Means

Wormwood is a plant found in the Middle East known for its bitter taste. Typically, wormwood is not a poisonous plant, but the result of the sounding of the third trumpet causes such devastation that the effect of wormwood becomes far more hazardous and destructive. Again, this is not an instant event, but occurs over a time period of three and a half years.

Revelation 8:9–11 Quiz Answers

1. What percentage of ships and living creatures in the sea were destroyed? C) one-third
2. When the third angel sounded its trumpet, what fell from heaven? A) a great star
3. What is Wormwood? B) a great star that fell from heaven

📖 REVELATION 8:12–13

Pre-Quiz

1. When the fourth angel sounded his trumpet, what was darkened?
   A. the light in heaven
   B. a third of the sun, a third of the moon, and a third of the stars
   C. the surface of the earth

2. A third of the day did not shine, but what happened to the night?
   A. It was completely black.
   B. A third of the night did not shine.
   C. It shone like the sun.

3. John looked and heard an angel flying through the midst of heaven, saying what word three times?
   A. Repent!
   B. Rejoice!
   C. Woe!

What the Scriptures Say (Revelation 8:12–13)

Then the fourth angel sounded: And a third of the sun was struck, a third of the moon, and a third of the stars, so that a third of them were darkened. A third of the day did not shine, and likewise the night. And I looked, and I heard an angel flying through the midst of heaven, saying with a loud voice, "Woe, woe, woe to the inhabitants of the earth, because of the remaining blasts of the trumpet of the three angels who are about to sound!"

What Revelation 8:12–13 Means

"Woe, woe, woe" refers to the impending final three trumpet judgments. The worst is yet to come. The first "woe" is the fifth trumpet, the second "woe" is the sixth trumpet, and the third "woe" is focused on Babylon, the Great Harlot, as we will discover later.

The results of the first four trumpets of mid-Tribulation:

- A third of the earth and its vegetation is charred and burned.
- A third of the sea can no longer provide a livable habitat for fish.
- A third of man's ships and shipping capabilities are destroyed.
- A third of the world's fresh water is poisoned.
- The sun, moon, and stars are affected by a natural upheaval, and a day becomes a mere sixteen hours.

Revelation 8:12–13 Quiz Answers

1. When the fourth angel sounded his trumpet, what was darkened?
   B) a third of the sun, a third of the moon, and a third of the stars
2. A third of the day did not shine, but what happened to the night? B)
   A third of the night did not shine.
3. John looked and heard an angel flying through the midst of heaven,
   saying what word three times? C) Woe!

REVELATION

9

LET MORE TRUMPETS SOUND

📖 REVELATION 9:1–4

Pre-Quiz

1. When the fifth angel sounded its trumpet, a key was given to the
   A. gates of heaven
   B. gates of hell
   C. bottomless pit

2. The sun and air were darkened because of
   A. a lack of the sun and moon
   B. smoke from the pit
   C. a wave of flies that filled the air

3. What was commanded to only harm men who do not have the seal of God on their foreheads?
   A. the angel of death
   B. the grim reaper
   C. locusts

What the Scriptures Say (Revelation 9:1)

Then the fifth angel sounded: And I saw a star fallen from heaven to the earth. To him was given the key to the bottomless pit.

What Revelation 9:1 Means

The sounding of the fifth trumpet initiates the first "woe." John did not see the star "fall" to earth; it had already fallen. The star is Satan, who was not in heaven at this time because he had already "fallen." Job 38:7 gives us precedence for stars being angels: ". . . when the morning stars sang together, and all the sons of God shouted for joy?"

What the Scriptures Say (Revelation 9:2)

And he opened the bottomless pit, and smoke arose out of the pit like the smoke of a great furnace. So the sun and the air were darkened because of the smoke of the pit.

What Revelation 9:2 Means

The bottomless pit of Revelation 9:2 is "the deep," or abyss. In Luke 8:30–31, a group of demons named Legion begged Jesus not to throw them into the abyss: "Jesus asked him, saying, 'What is your name?' And he said, 'Legion,' because many demons had entered him. And they begged Him that He would not command them to go out into the abyss."

The abyss serves as a spiritual, maximum-security prison for some demons and the place where Satan will be bound during Jesus Christ's reign, as we will learn later in Revelation.

What the Scriptures Say (Revelation 9:3–4)

Then out of the smoke locusts came upon the earth. And to them was given power, as the scorpions of the earth have power. They were commanded not to harm the grass of the earth, or any green thing, or any tree, but only those men who do not have the seal of God on their foreheads.

What Revelation 9:3–4 Means

The locusts that spew from the smoke of the abyss are empowered to be especially dangerous. However, God is still completely in control, causing the locusts to avoid their natural attraction to crops and anyone with the seal of God. These horrifying locusts will attack unbelieving people who have shunned God.

Revelation 9:1–4 Quiz Answers

1. When the fifth angel sounded its trumpet, a key was given to the C) bottomless pit.
2. The sun and air were darkened because of B) smoke from the pit.
3. What was commanded to only harm men who do not have the seal of God on their foreheads? C) locusts

📖 REVELATION 9:5–11

Pre-Quiz

1. How long were many to be tormented like the torment of a scorpion when it strikes a man?
   A. one week
   B. five months
   C. seven years

2. In those days, what would men seek but not be able to find?
   A. relief
   B. forgiveness
   C. death

3. What is the name of the angel of the bottomless pit?
   A. Abaddon
   B. Lucifer
   C. Wrath

What the Scriptures Say (Revelation 9:5–11)

And they were not given authority to kill them, but to torment them for five months. Their torment was like the torment of a scorpion when it strikes a man. In those days men will seek death and will not find it; they will desire to die, and death will flee from them. The shape of the locusts was like horses prepared for battle. On their heads were crowns of something like gold, and their faces were like the faces of men. They had hair like women's hair, and their teeth were like lions' teeth. And they had breastplates like breastplates of iron, and the sound of their wings was like the sound of chariots with many horses running into battle. They had tails like scorpions, and there were stings in their tails. Their power was to hurt men five months. And they had as king over them the angel of the bottomless pit, whose name in Hebrew is Abaddon, but in Greek he has the name Apollyon.

What Revelation 9:5–11 Means

For five months, anguish will rule on earth as gruesome, swarming locusts "torment" the unbelievers. Under God's restrictions, but under the command of the angel of the bottomless pit, the locusts are not allowed to kill, but are permitted to torment.

The sting of a scorpion is very painful, and men will be so agonized that they will yearn for death to end their misery, but they will not be able to die. Besides pain, scorpion stings bring on other symptoms, such as rapid breathing, muscle twitching, and overall weakness.

An interesting note is that the five-month period of torment corresponds to the life span of locusts—about five months.

The angel of the bottomless pit, Abaddon, which translates to "Destruction," is Satan. It is Satan controlling the demonic locusts, but as always, God is more powerful and prohibits Satan from using the locusts to cause death.

Revelation 9:5–11 Quiz Answers

1. How long were many to be tormented like the torment of a scorpion when it strikes a man? B) five months

2. In those days, what would men seek but not be able to find? C) death

3. What is the name of the angel of the bottomless pit? A) Abaddon

📖 REVELATION 9:12–18

Pre-Quiz

1. When the sixth angel sounded its trumpet, John heard a voice from who or what?

    A. four elders collectively

    B. four horns of a golden altar

    C. Jesus Himself

2. What was the number of the army of the horsemen?

    A. multitudes upon multitudes

    B. 144,000

    C. 200 million

3. How many plagues killed a third of mankind?

    A. three

    B. seven

    C. twelve

What the Scriptures Say (Revelation 9:12)

One woe is past. Behold, still two more woes are coming after these things.

What Revelation 9:12 Means

The first woe, the plague of demonic locusts, is over. The second of the three woes is about to come.

What the Scriptures Say (Revelation 9:13)

Then the sixth angel sounded: And I heard a voice from the four horns of the golden altar which is before God.

What Revelation 9:13 Means

The voice John hears is the voice of Jesus. The voice is singular, not a harmony of voices as of the martyrs, and the voice gives a command. There is no mention of the voice being of an angel as in previous passages, therefore all indications point to the voice being that of Jesus Christ Himself.

What the Scriptures Say (Revelation 9:14–15)

. . . saying to the sixth angel who had the trumpet, "Release the four angels who are bound at the great river Euphrates." So the four angels, who had been prepared for the hour and day and month and year, were released to kill a third of mankind.

What Revelation 9:14–15 Means

Four angels, obviously fallen angels or there would have been no need to have them bound, are finally released from the great river Euphrates, which is the border on the eastern side of the land promised to Abraham and his descendants. Genesis 15:18 reads, "On the same day the LORD made a covenant with Abram, saying: 'To your descendants I have given this land, from the river of Egypt to the great river, the River Euphrates.'"

Reading carefully, we find that "the hour and day and month and year" (roughly thirteen months) refers not to the amount of time the four fallen angels were being prepared for release, but rather to the time span they have been given to do their evil work. Therefore, the four fallen angels will kill one-third of mankind during a thirteen-month period.

The mission of the released angels is to kill one-third of mankind. The exactness of the time selected to release the four fallen angels is further indication of the infinite power of God and the preciseness and accuracy of His control. It also shows the limitations of Satan, who was not able to override God's directives and free the angels prematurely.

With the fourth seal judgment of Revelation 6:8 reducing the earth's population by one-fourth, and now the sixth trumpet judgment reducing the earth's population by one-third, one-half of the earth's population has now been destroyed.

What the Scriptures Say (Revelation 9:16–18)

Now the number of the army of the horsemen was two hundred million; I heard the number of them. And thus I saw the horses in the vision: those who sat on them had breastplates of fiery red, hyacinth blue, and sulfur yellow; and the heads of the horses were like the heads of lions; and out of their mouths came fire, smoke, and brimstone. By these three plagues a third of mankind was killed—by the fire and the smoke and the brimstone which came out of their mouths.

What Revelation 9:16–18 Means

This is not a geographical region within the one-fourth of the earth under control of the Antichrist, which means this army is not under the direction of the Antichrist, but is a separate unit altogether.

Revelation 9:12–18 Quiz Answers

1. When the sixth angel sounded its trumpet, John heard a voice from who or what? B) four horns of a golden altar
2. What was the number of the army of the horsemen? C) 200 million
3. How many plagues killed a third of mankind? A) three

📖 REVELATION 9:19–21

Pre-Quiz

1. The rest of mankind who were not killed by plagues did not
   A. bow down
   B. repent
   C. continue in their wicked ways

2. The rest of mankind continued to worship
   A. Jesus
   B. all sorts of idols
   C. themselves

3. The statement that men did not repent of their murders is
   A. true
   B. somewhat true
   C. false

What the Scriptures Say (Revelation 9:19–21)

For their power is in their mouth and in their tails; for their tails are like serpents, having heads; and with them they do harm. But the rest of mankind, who were not killed by these plagues, did not repent of the works of their hands, that they should not worship demons, and idols of gold, silver, brass, stone, and wood, which can neither see nor hear nor walk. And they did not repent of their murders or their sorceries or their sexual immorality or their thefts.

What Revelation 9:19–21 Means

The fact that the rest of mankind still did not repent, despite the plagues and unimaginable atrocities, is remindful of hard-hearted Pharaoh and his stubbornness during the plagues cast upon Egypt in the book of Exodus: "Then Pharaoh sent, and indeed, not even one of the livestock of the Israelites was dead. But the heart of Pharaoh became hard, and he did not let the people go" (9:7). Despite incredible devastation, at this time mankind still did not repent and accept Jesus as Lord.

An underlying fact not to be missed is that now, deep into the Tribulation, there was still a chance for mankind to repent, although they choose to reject the opportunity. Mankind did not repent from grievous sins such as murder, sexual immorality, thievery, and sorcery, which includes numerology, witchcraft, and horoscope-related astrological indulgence.

Revelation 9:19–21 Quiz Answers

1. The rest of mankind who were not killed by plagues did not B) repent.
2. The rest of mankind continued to worship B) all sorts of idols.
3. The statement that men did not repent of their murders is A) true.

REVELATION

10

AFTER THE SEVENTH
SEAL IS OPENED

📖 REVELATION 10:1–4

Pre-Quiz

1. John saw a mighty angel coming from heaven clothed with a
   A. sword
   B. tunic
   C. cloud

2. When the angel cried out, what uttered their voices?
   A. seven angels
   B. seven lions
   C. seven thunders

3. After hearing the voices, John was about to write. But he was told
   A. bow down and worship
   B. do not write
   C. sing and rejoice

What the Scriptures Say (Revelation 10:1–4)

I saw still another mighty angel coming down from heaven, clothed with a cloud. And a rainbow was on his head, his face was like the sun, and his feet like pillars of fire. He had a little book open in his hand. And he set his right foot on the sea and his left foot on the land, and cried with a loud voice, as when a lion roars. When he cried out, seven thunders uttered their voices. Now when the seven thunders uttered their voices, I was about to write; but I heard a voice from heaven saying to me, "Seal up the things which the seven thunders uttered, and do not write them."

What Revelation 10:1–4 Means

This spectacular "mighty angel" is not Christ. Christ is not an angel, nor does He come to earth before the end of the Tribulation.

Revelation 10:1–4 Quiz Answers

1. John saw a mighty angel coming from heaven clothed with a C) cloud.
2. When the angel cried out, what uttered their voices? C) seven thunders
3. After hearing the voices, John was about to write. But he was told B) do not write.

📖 REVELATION 10:5–11

Pre-Quiz

1. According to John, when the seventh angel is about to sound its trumpet, the mystery of God would be
   A. revealed
   B. finished
   C. about to begin

2. When John asked the angel to give him the little book, the angel told him to
   A. finish writing
   B. stop talking
   C. take it and eat it

3. What did John do with the little book?
   A. He burned it.
   B. He ate it.
   C. He cast it into the sea.

What the Scriptures Say (Revelation 10:5–11)

The angel whom I saw standing on the sea and on the land raised up his hand to heaven and swore by Him who lives forever and ever, who created heaven and the things that are in it, the earth and the things that are in it, and the sea and the things that are in it, that there should be delay no longer, but in the days of the sounding of the seventh angel, when he is about to sound, the mystery of God would be finished, as He declared to His servants the prophets. Then the voice which I heard from heaven spoke to me again and said, "Go, take the little book which is open in the hand of the angel who stands on the sea and on the earth."

So I went to the angel and said to him, "Give me the little book."

And he said to me, "Take and eat it; and it will make your stomach bitter, but it will be as sweet as honey in your mouth."

Then I took the little book out of the angel's hand and ate it, and it was as sweet as honey in my mouth. But when I had eaten it, my stomach became bitter. And he said to me, "You must prophesy again about many peoples, nations, tongues, and kings."

What Revelation 10:5–11 Means

The angel in verse 5 is not Jesus Christ. The delay is over, and the end times are rapidly approaching. When the seventh angel's trumpet sounds, the entire world moves forward toward the complete fulfillment of the Bible's prophecies. The climax will be the return of Jesus Christ to earth.

"Eating the book" is symbolic, not literal. It means to "digest" the contents of the book or scroll. We have reference to this in Jeremiah 15:16: "Your words were found, and I ate them, and Your word was to me the joy and rejoicing of my heart; for I am called by Your name, O LORD God of hosts."

To be a spokesperson for God, there is a prerequisite of "digesting" His Word.

QUICK FACT: When we read "mystery," it typically refers to something God will reveal that humans could not possibly comprehend without His Word. The mysteries of God can only be properly revealed by God Himself.

Revelation 10:5–11 Quiz Answers

1. According to John, when the seventh angel is about to sound its trumpet, the mystery of God would be B) finished.
2. When John asked the angel to give him the little book, the angel told him to C) take it and eat it.
3. What did John do with the little book? B) He ate it.

REVELATION

11

THE BETRAYAL OF THE ANTICHRIST

📖 REVELATION 11:1–3

Pre-Quiz

1. What was John told to measure?
   A. the length of Patmos
   B. the temple of God
   C. New Jerusalem

2. How long will the holy city be tread underfoot?
   A. 40 days and 40 nights
   B. 42 months
   C. 40 years

3. How long will the two witnesses prophesy?

   A. 90 days

   B. 120 days

   C. 1,260 days

What the Scriptures Say (Revelation 11:1–3)

Then I was given a reed like a measuring rod. And the angel stood, saying, "Rise and measure the temple of God, the altar, and those who worship there. But leave out the court which is outside the temple, and do not measure it, for it has been given to the Gentiles. And they will tread the holy city underfoot for forty-two months. And I will give power to my two witnesses, and they will prophesy one thousand two hundred and sixty days, clothed in sackcloth."

What Revelation 11:1–3 Means

During the last three and a half years of the Tribulation, the holy city will be controlled by Gentiles under the direct supervision of the Antichrist. It is during this time that the Antichrist will promote himself as God.

God's two dynamic witnesses will prophesy for 1,260 days. The two witnesses are Jews whose goal is to minister to Israel. They have supernatural powers and will warn the world that a judgment is coming.

Revelation 11:1–3 Quiz Answers

1. What was John told to measure? B) the temple of God
2. How long will the holy city be tread underfoot? B) 42 months
3. How long will the two witnesses prophesy? C) 1,260 days

📖 REVELATION 11:4–9

Pre-Quiz

1. What would happen if anyone harms the two olive trees and two lampstands standing before God?
    A. Fire would proceed from their mouths.
    B. The mountains would tremble.
    C. The skies would turn fiery red.

2. What is the name of the great city mentioned in Revelation 11:8?
    A. Babylon
    B. New Jerusalem
    C. Sodom and Egypt

3. How long will the nations see dead bodies?
    A. three days and three nights
    B. three and a half days
    C. for all eternity

What the Scriptures Say (Revelation 11:4–9)

These are the two olive trees and the two lampstands standing before the God of the earth. And if anyone wants to harm them, fire proceeds from their mouth and devours their enemies. And if anyone wants to harm them, he must be killed in this manner. These have power to shut heaven, so that no rain falls in the days of their prophecy; and they have power over waters to turn them to blood, and to strike the earth with all plagues, as often as they desire. When they finish their testimony, the beast that ascends out of the bottomless pit will make war against them, overcome them, and kill them. And their dead bodies will lie in the street of the great city which spiritually is called Sodom and Egypt, where also our Lord was crucified. Then those from the peoples, tribes, tongues, and nations will see their dead bodies three-and-a-half days, and not allow their dead bodies to be put into graves.

What Revelation 11:4–9 Means

God has given the two witnesses power, including the ability to devour their enemies with fire. They can also prevent the heavens from raining, causing a tremendous drought upon the earth. Because of their supernatural abilities, it is apparent to anyone and everyone that these two witnesses have been sent by God.

After the 1,260 days, the Antichrist is allowed to murder them. Leaving their bodies in the streets for three days, the evil Antichrist becomes the most dominant figure on earth.

Because of the far reach of technology, "nations" see the dead bodies for three and a half days, and forbid the bodies to be put into graves. Pure hatred toward the two witnesses and the almighty God will be a reason of celebration over the earth, as the two witnesses who warned the world to repent are silenced.

Revelation 11:4–9 Quiz Answers

1. What would happen if anyone harms the two olive trees and two lampstands standing before God? A) Fire would proceed from their mouths.
2. What is the name of the great city mentioned in Revelation 11:8? C) Sodom and Egypt
3. How long will the nations see dead bodies? B) three and a half days

📖 REVELATION 11:10–16

Pre-Quiz

1. How many prophets tormented those who would dwell on the earth?
   A. one
   B. two
   C. four

2. In Revelation 11:13, when a great earthquake rocked the city, how much of it fell?
   A. half
   B. one-tenth
   C. all of it

3. When the seventh angel sounded its trumpet, who fell on their faces and worshiped God?
   A. the twenty-four elders
   B. all the stars in the sky
   C. the witnesses

What the Scriptures Say (Revelation 11:10–16)

And those who dwell on the earth will rejoice over them, make merry, and send gifts to one another, because these two prophets tormented those who dwell on the earth. Now after the three-and-a-half days the breath of life from God entered them, and they stood on their feet, and great fear fell on those who saw them. And they heard a loud voice from heaven saying to them, "Come up here." And they ascended to heaven in a cloud, and their enemies saw them. In the same hour there was a great earthquake, and a tenth of the city fell. In the earthquake seven thousand people were killed, and the rest were afraid and gave glory to the God of heaven.

The second woe is past. Behold, the third woe is coming quickly.

Then the seventh angel sounded: And there were loud voices in heaven, saying, "The kingdoms of this world have become the kingdoms of our Lord and of His Christ, and He shall reign forever and ever!" And the twenty-four elders who sat before God on their thrones fell on their faces and worshiped God.

What Revelation 11:10–16 Means

After three and a half days, God breathes life into the two dead bodies of the witnesses. The mere sight of this prompts enormous fear in everyone aware of this miracle. The two witnesses are resurrected supernaturally and are sent into heaven in a cloud. This "rapture" creates fear and trembling and a newfound awe for the almighty God.

Now, many thousands who mocked and jeered the two witnesses and celebrated their deaths reverse themselves and put their faith in the Lord, becoming "little children," then "young men [or women]," and then "fathers" in that they "have known Him who is from the beginning" (1 John 2:12–14).

As with all new converts to Christ, the five ways of using the Word for spiritual nutrition are to

1. hear it.
2. read it.
3. study it.
4. memorize it.
5. meditate on it.

For it is written, "Man shall not live by bread alone, but by every word that proceeds from the mouth of God" (Matt. 4:4).

Revelation 11:10–16 Quiz Answers

1. How many prophets tormented those who would dwell on the earth? B) two
2. In Revelation 11:13, when a great earthquake rocked the city, how much of it fell? B) one-tenth
3. When the seventh angel sounded its trumpet, who fell on their faces and worshiped God? A) the twenty-four elders

📖 REVELATION 11:17–19

Pre-Quiz

1. According to Revelation 11:18, the nations were full of
   A. faith
   B. wrath
   C. vengeance

2. The time had come for the judging of the
   A. kings of the earth
   B. dead
   C. Antichrist

3. Where was the temple of God opened?
   A. among the clouds
   B. in heaven
   C. on earth

What the Scriptures Say (Revelation 11:17–19)

. . . saying:

> "We give You thanks, O Lord God Almighty,
> The One who is and who was and who is to come,
> Because You have taken Your great power and reigned.
> The nations were angry, and Your wrath has come,
> And the time of the dead, that they should be judged,
> And that You should reward Your servants the prophets and the
> saints,
> And those who fear Your name, small and great,
> And should destroy those who destroy the earth."

Then the temple of God was opened in heaven, and the ark of His covenant was seen in His temple. And there were lightnings, noises, thunderings, an earthquake, and great hail.

What Revelation 11:17–19 Means

Verses 17–19 refer to the twenty-four elders in heaven. The elders rejoice mightily, singing a song of thanksgiving at the glory of the Lord and the fact that God's judgment is at the halfway point, only three and a half years from completion.

The ark of His covenant is not the same as the ark of the covenant on earth. Rather, it was the heavenly ark from which the earthly ark was modeled.

Revelation 11:17–19 Quiz Answers

1. According to Revelation 11:18, the nations were full of B) wrath.
2. The time had come for the judging of the B) dead.
3. Where was the temple of God opened? B) in heaven

REVELATION

CLOTHED IN THE SUN

📖 REVELATION 12:1–4

Pre-Quiz

1. The great signs in the heavens included a woman clothed with
   A. the sun
   B. a shroud
   C. a royal headdress

2. There was something very special about the woman. She was
   A. gigantic
   B. pregnant
   C. symbolic

3. What ghastly thing stood before the woman?
   A. the devil
   B. a red dragon
   C. a mighty circuit

What the Scriptures Say (Revelation 12:1–4)

Now a great sign appeared in heaven: a woman clothed with the sun, with the moon under her feet, and on her head a garland of twelve stars. Then being with child, she cried out in labor and in pain to give birth. And another sign appeared in heaven: behold, a great, fiery red dragon having seven heads and ten horns, and seven diadems on his heads. His tail drew a third of the stars of heaven and threw them to the earth. And the dragon stood before the woman who was ready to give birth, to devour her Child as soon as it was born.

What Revelation 12:1–4 Means

Revelation 12 begins the middle of the Tribulation. The nation of Israel will be despised more now than at any other time in its history.

For the first time in the book of Revelation, we see the word "sign." Since the woman in verse 1 is called "a great sign [that] appeared in heaven," we know the woman represents something other than a female person. In addition, it is believed by some that this woman is the Virgin Mary. But verse 2 has the "woman" with child, and Mary gave birth on earth, not in heaven, therefore this woman could not possibly be the Virgin Mary.

The red dragon of verse 3 is Satan. The "seven heads" represent seven world kingdoms from Assyria, Babylon, Greece, Rome, Egypt, Medo-Persia, and a government of the Antichrist that consists of "ten horns."

Revelation 12:1–4 Quiz Answers

1. The great signs in the heavens included a woman clothed with A) the sun.
2. There was something very special about the woman. She was B) pregnant.
3. What ghastly thing stood before the woman? B) a red dragon

📖 REVELATION 12:5–8

Pre-Quiz

1. The child born to the woman would
    A. rule all nations
    B. cause her great grief
    C. be the downfall of the heavens

2. The woman fled to a place prepared by
    A. her son
    B. God
    C. Satan

3. During the war in heaven, who fought the dragon?
    A. the once-pregnant woman
    B. the angel Michael
    C. the four elders

What the Scriptures Say (Revelation 12:5–8)

She bore a male Child who was to rule all nations with a rod of iron. And her Child was caught up to God and His throne. Then the woman fled into the wilderness, where she has a place prepared by God, that they should feed her there one thousand two hundred and sixty days. And war broke out in heaven: Michael and his angels fought with the dragon; and the dragon and his angels fought, but they did not prevail, nor was a place found for them in heaven any longer.

What Revelation 12:5–8 Means

During this time period, Satan's attack and persecution of Israel will be horrific. It will be more devastating and evil than the Holocaust. Yet, God remains faithful.

This is what the Hebrew prophets warned was coming in passages such as Leviticus 26:40–45:

But if they confess their iniquity and the iniquity of their fathers, with their unfaithfulness in which they were unfaithful to Me, and that they also have walked contrary to Me, and that I also have walked contrary to them and have brought them into the land of their enemies; if their uncircumcised hearts are humbled, and they accept their guilt—then I will remember My covenant with Jacob, and My covenant with Isaac and My covenant with Abraham I will remember; I will remember the land. The land also shall be left empty by them, and will enjoy its sabbaths while it lies desolate without them; they will accept their guilt, because they despised My judgments and because their soul abhorred My statutes. Yet for all that, when they are in the land of their enemies, I will not cast them away, nor shall I abhor them, to utterly destroy them and break My covenant with them; for I am the LORD their God. But for their sake I will remember the covenant of their ancestors, whom I brought out of the land of Egypt in the sight of the nations, that I might be their God: I am the LORD.

In addition, Jeremiah 23:3–8 reads:

"But I will gather the remnant of My flock out of all countries where I have driven them, and bring them back to their folds; and they shall be fruitful and increase. I will set up shepherds over them who will feed them; and they shall fear no more, nor be dismayed, nor shall they be lacking," says the LORD.

"Behold, the days are coming," says the LORD,
"That I will raise to David a Branch of righteousness;
A King shall reign and prosper,
And execute judgment and righteousness in the earth.
In His days Judah will be saved,
And Israel will dwell safely;
Now this is His name by which He will be called:

THE LORD OUR RIGHTEOUSNESS.

"Therefore, behold, the days are coming," says the LORD, "that they shall no longer say, 'As the LORD lives who brought up the children of Israel from the land of Egypt,' but, 'As the LORD lives who brought up and led the descendants of the house of Israel from the north country and from all the countries where I had driven them.' And they shall dwell in their own land."

Verse 7 tells of a war that breaks out in heaven. The fierce war is between the forces of evil, Satan, and Michael the archangel. This description of war deals with Satan's fall, which happened centuries ago. With limited access to God, Satan becomes a great accuser of the brethren, as he accused Job and countless others from that day to this day.

Revelation 12:5–8 Quiz Answers

1. The child born to the woman would A) rule all nations.
2. The woman fled to a place prepared by B) God.
3. During the war in heaven, who fought the dragon? B) the angel Michael

📖 REVELATION 12:9–12

Pre-Quiz

1. What did John see coming from the sea?
   A. a beast
   B. the sun
   C. a great fish

2. What happened to the accuser of our brothers?
   A. He was set ablaze.
   B. He was cast down.
   C. He began to accuse our sisters as well.

3. Revelation 12:12 casts woe to the inhabitants of
   A. the earth
   B. the heavens
   C. the devil's empire

What the Scriptures Say (Revelation 12:9–12)

So the great dragon was cast out, that serpent of old, called the Devil and Satan, who deceives the whole world; he was cast to the earth, and his angels were cast out with him.

Then I heard a loud voice saying in heaven, "Now salvation, and strength, and the kingdom of our God, and the power of His Christ have come, for the accuser of our brethren, who accused them before our God day and night, has been cast down. And they overcame him by the blood of the Lamb and by the word of their testimony, and they did not love their lives to the death. Therefore rejoice, O heavens, and you who dwell in them! Woe to the inhabitants of the earth and the sea! For the devil has come down to you, having great wrath, because he knows that he has a short time."

What Revelation 12:9–12 Means

"That serpent of old" harkens back to the longtime evil of Satan, recalling Satan's temptation of Eve in the garden of Eden. Here, there is no possible room for misinterpretation, as the serpent is clearly called "Satan" and "the Devil."

Now, in the final three and a half years of the Tribulation, Satan releases his most vicious attack ever on mankind. He realizes he has only a short time left. Jesus Himself alerted us to the fact that this would be the greatest trial of the Tribulation in Matthew 24:21: "For then there will be great tribulation, such as has not been since the beginning of the world until this time, no, nor ever shall be."

Revelation 12:9–12 Quiz Answers

1. What did John see coming from the sea? A) a beast
2. What happened to the accuser of our brothers? B) He was cast down.
3. Revelation 12:12 casts woe to the inhabitants of A) the earth.

📖 REVELATION 12:13–17

Pre-Quiz

1. When cast to the earth, who did the dragon persecute?
   A. the woman who bore the child
   B. its fallen angels
   C. the people of the earth

2. What helped the woman?
   A. a mighty wind
   B. a hurricane
   C. an eagle

3. What good thing became of the woman's seed?
   A. It remained faithful to the woman.
   B. It repented in earnest.
   C. It kept the commandments of God.

What the Scriptures Say (Revelation 12:13–17)

Now when the dragon saw that he had been cast to the earth, he persecuted the woman who gave birth to the male Child. But the woman was
given two wings of a great eagle, that she might fly into the wilderness to
her place, where she is nourished for a time and times and half a time,
from the presence of the serpent. So the serpent spewed water out of his
mouth like a flood after the woman, that he might cause her to be carried
away by the flood. But the earth helped the woman, and the earth opened
its mouth and swallowed up the flood which the dragon had spewed out
of his mouth. And the dragon was enraged with the woman, and he went
to make war with the rest of her offspring, who keep the commandments
of God and have the testimony of Jesus Christ.

What Revelation 12:13–17 Means

The serpent represents the devil. The woman represents Israel and the Israelites, who have now accepted Jesus Christ as their Messiah and are fleeing the Antichrist.

The offspring of the woman, who Satan and the Antichrist both want to conquer and destroy, is symbolic of the Jews who have worshiped Jesus as their Lord and Savior.

Revelation 12:13–17 Quiz Answers

1. When cast to the earth, who did the dragon persecute? A) the woman who bore the child
2. What helped the woman? C) an eagle
3. What good thing became of the woman's seed? C) It kept the commandments of God.

REVELATION

THE TWO BEASTS

📖 REVELATION 13:1–4

Pre-Quiz

1. What was on the horns of the beast with seven heads?
   A. deadly vines
   B. ten crowns
   C. ten olives

2. The beast that John saw in Revelation 13 was like a
   A. tiger
   B. dragon
   C. leopard

3. Who worshiped the dragon that gave authority to the beast?
   A. all the earth
   B. the warriors on red horses
   C. the serpents of the sea

How does Daniel's vision compare with John's vision in Revelation 13?

The table below demonstrates how a great deal of Bible prophecy can be understood by comparing Revelation with the Old Testament, and the book of Daniel in particular. It is very important to understand who the major players are in so much of the prophecy revealed in Revelation.

Daniel 12:4 says, "But you, Daniel, shut up the words, and seal the book until the time of the end; many shall run to and fro, and knowledge shall increase."

Power of the Antichrist From Daniel Chapter 7	Power of the Antichrist From Revelation Chapter 13
Four beasts from the sea—verse 3	Four beasts from the sea—verses 1 and 2
Lion—verse 4	Lion—verse 2
Bear—verse 5	Bear—verse 2
Leopard—verse 6	Leopard—verse 2
Beast with ten horns—verse 7	Beast with ten horns—verse 1
Mouth speaking pompous words—verse 8	Mouth speaking pompous words—verse 5
Waging war with the saints—verse 21	Waging war with the saints—verse 7
Power for 42 months (3.5 years)—verse 25	Power for 42 months—verse 5

What the Scriptures Say (Revelation 13:1–4)

Then I stood on the sand of the sea. And I saw a beast rising up out of the sea, having seven heads and ten horns, and on his horns ten crowns, and on his heads a blasphemous name. Now the beast which I saw was like a leopard, his feet were like the feet of a bear, and his mouth like the mouth of a lion. The dragon gave him his power, his throne, and great authority. And I saw one of his heads as if it had been mortally wounded, and his deadly wound was healed. And all the world marveled and followed the beast. So they worshiped the dragon who gave authority to the beast; and they worshiped the beast, saying, "Who is like the beast? Who is able to make war with him?"

What Revelation 13:1–4 Means

The evil beast out of the sea is one of the most prevailing characters during the final three and a half years of the Tribulation. "Blasphemous name" indicates that the Antichrist and his kingdom are strictly and unapologetically against God.

Midway through the Tribulation, the Antichrist will be killed. Its body, before it can be buried, will be physically invaded by Satan. Now, Satan will have power over all the world.

Revelation 13:1–4 Quiz Answers

1. What was on the horns of the beast with seven heads? B) ten crowns
2. The beast that John saw in Revelation 13 was like a C) leopard.
3. Who worshiped the dragon that gave authority to the beast? A) all the earth

📖 REVELATION 13:5–11

Pre-Quiz

1. Authority was given to the creature to continue for
   A. forty days and forty nights
   B. forty-two months
   C. seven years

2. Complete this sentence: If anyone will kill with the sword
   A. he himself will be beheaded
   B. he will be thrown into the pit
   C. he must be killed by the sword

3. The beast that had two horns like a lamb spoke like a
   A. lamb
   B. dragon
   C. harp

What the Scriptures Say (Revelation 13:5–11)

And he was given a mouth speaking great things and blasphemies, and he was given authority to continue for forty-two months. Then he opened his mouth in blasphemy against God, to blaspheme His name, His tabernacle, and those who dwell in heaven. It was granted to him to make war with the saints and to overcome them. And authority was given him over every tribe, tongue, and nation. All who dwell on the earth will worship him, whose names have not been written in the Book of Life of the Lamb slain from the foundation of the world. If anyone has an ear, let him hear. He who leads into captivity shall go into captivity; he who kills with the sword must be killed with the sword. Here is the patience and the faith of the saints. Then I saw another beast coming up out of the earth, and he had two horns like a lamb and spoke like a dragon.

What Revelation 13:5–11 Means

This creature, this "beast," which is the Antichrist, not only reviles God and blasphemes Him but also reviles all that are in heaven. During this time, Satan will be worshiped by practically everyone upon the earth. However, no believers in Jesus Christ will worship the Antichrist. Their names are written "in the Book of Life of the Lamb," and they are all those who have called on the name of Jesus for salvation.

Verse 10 refers to those saints who bravely and staunchly endure while being persecuted for their faith.

Verse 11 marks the arrival of a second "beast." He is a constant companion of the Antichrist and will become the head of the religions of the world, as we will learn in Revelation 17. Because the second beast has "two horns like a lamb," he will appear as a wolf in sheep's clothing. He will teach a false gospel that supports the Antichrist's doctrine. He is a liar and is out to destroy men's souls.

Revelation 13:5–11 Quiz Answers

1. Authority was given to the creature to continue for B) forty-two months.

2. Complete this sentence: If anyone will kill with the sword C) he must be killed by the sword.

3. The beast that had two horns like a lamb, spoke like a B) dragon.

📖 REVELATION 13:12–18

Pre-Quiz

1. What happened to the wound of the first beast?
   A. It grew.
   B. It healed.
   C. It killed it.

2. Where did both rich and poor receive a mark?
   A. on their tongues
   B. on their foreheads or right hands
   C. on their palms

3. What is the number of the Beast?
   A. 363
   B. 666
   C. 999

What the Scriptures Say (Revelation 13:12–18)

And he exercises all the authority of the first beast in his presence, and causes the earth and those who dwell in it to worship the first beast, whose deadly wound was healed. He performs great signs, so that he even makes fire come down from heaven on the earth in the sight of men. And he deceives those who dwell on the earth by those signs which he was granted to do in the sight of the beast, telling those who dwell on the earth to make an image to the beast who was wounded by the sword and lived. He was granted power to give breath to the image of the beast, that the image of the beast should both speak and cause as many as would not worship the image of the beast to be killed. He causes all, both small and great, rich and poor, free and slave, to receive a mark on their right hand or on their foreheads, and that no one may buy or sell except one who has the mark or the name of the beast, or the number of his name. Here is wisdom. Let him who has understanding calculate the number of the beast, for it is the number of a man: His number is 666.

What Revelation 13:12–18 Means

This "False Prophet," as second in command, will have the world worshiping the Antichrist by forceful means. The False Prophet's ability to bring fire from heaven will support his deception, as those who dwell upon the earth will see his supernatural abilities. The False Prophet's power is stronger than that of the false prophets of Baal who tried but were unsuccessful in calling down fire in the days of Elisha as written in 1 Kings 18:36–38:

And it came to pass, at the time of the offering of the evening sacrifice, that Elijah the prophet came near and said, "Lord God of Abraham, Isaac, and Israel, let it be known this day that You are God in Israel and I am Your servant, and that I have done all these things at Your word. Hear me, O Lord, hear me, that this people may know that You are the Lord God, and that You have turned their hearts back to You again." Then the fire of the Lord fell and consumed the burnt sacrifice, and the wood and the stones and the dust, and it licked up the water that was in the trench.

Because the False Prophet exhibits such power, many will believe in the Antichrist.

Verse 15 teaches that similar to what Nebuchadnezzar did, the False Prophet will have an image of the Antichrist constructed, in order for people to worship the image. Incredibly, the image will appear to be alive.

The False Prophet will require all people to have "the mark of the beast." This will bring the entire world into one government with one economy and one religion. Without the mark of the Beast on either one's forehead or right hand, no one will be able to buy or sell goods.

Back in Revelation 13:8, it is revealed that some will refuse to worship the Antichrist. They will not have the mark upon them.

The mark of the Beast is 666. Without this mark, it is virtually impossible for those upon the earth to survive, humanly speaking . . . or without divine intervention, but they will be delivered:

> And it shall come to pass afterward
> That I will pour out My Spirit on all flesh;
> Your sons and your daughters shall prophesy,
> Your old men shall dream dreams,
> Your young men shall see visions.
> And also on My menservants and on My maidservants
> I will pour out My Spirit in those days.
> And I will show wonders in the heavens and in the earth:
> Blood and fire and pillars of smoke.
> The sun shall be turned into darkness,
> And the moon into blood,
> Before the coming of the great and awesome day of the LORD.
> And it shall come to pass
> That whoever calls on the name of the LORD
> Shall be saved.
> For in Mount Zion and in Jerusalem there shall be deliverance,
> As the LORD has said,
> Among the remnant whom the LORD calls. (Joel 2:28–32)

Revelation 13:12–18 Quiz Answers

1. What happened to the wound of the first beast? B) It healed.
2. Where did both rich and poor receive a mark? B) on their foreheads or right hands
3. What is the number of the Beast? B) 666

REVELATION

14

GOD PREPARES FOR
HIS JUDGMENT

📖 REVELATION 14:1–5

Pre-Quiz

1. John looked, and what did he see standing on Mount Zion?
    A. the lion
    B. the Lamb
    C. the dragon

2. John heard the voice that sounded like many instruments. Which instruments?
    A. harps
    B. violins
    C. drums

3. Who were the only ones who could learn a new song before the throne?

A. the last faithful

B. the 144,000 who were redeemed

C. the kings of the earth

What the Scriptures Say (Revelation 14:1–5)

Then I looked, and behold, a Lamb standing on Mount Zion, and with Him one hundred and forty-four thousand, having His Father's name written on their foreheads. And I heard a voice from heaven, like the voice of many waters, and like the voice of loud thunder. And I heard the sound of harpists playing their harps. They sang as it were a new song before the throne, before the four living creatures, and the elders; and no one could learn that song except the hundred and forty-four thousand who were redeemed from the earth. These are the ones who were not defiled with women, for they are virgins. These are the ones who follow the Lamb wherever He goes. These were redeemed from among men, being first-fruits to God and to the Lamb. And in their mouth was found no deceit, for they are without fault before the throne of God.

What Revelation 14:1–5 Means

The 144,000 mentioned in verse 1 are not the same 144,000 mentioned in Revelation 7. The latter 144,000 are devoted followers of Christ who were standing before the throne of God. The location must be heaven because according to John, the Lamb was standing on Mount Zion. The only definitions for Mount Zion in the Bible are as the earthly site of Jerusalem and the heavenly site of Jerusalem. Jesus would not be on the earth during this Tribulation period, therefore Scripture is speaking of the heavenly Mount Zion.

There is another mention of this heavenly Jerusalem, Mount Zion, in Hebrews 12:22–24:

But you have come to Mount Zion and to the city of the living God, the heavenly Jerusalem, to an innumerable company of angels, to the general assembly and church of the firstborn who are registered in heaven, to God the Judge of all, to the spirits of just men made perfect, to Jesus the Mediator of the new covenant, and to the blood of sprinkling that speaks better things than that of Abel.

The 144,000 from Revelation 7 were from the tribes of Israel, and their activity was on earth. Also, the group from Revelation 7 is sealed with the seal of the Father, while the Revelation 14 group has upon their heads the name of both the Father and the Son. This leaves little doubt that the groups are separate.

Revelation 14:1–5 Quiz Answers
1. John looked, and what did he see standing on Mount Zion? B) the Lamb
2. John heard the voice that sounded like many instruments. Which instruments? A) harps
3. Who were the only ones who could learn a new song before the throne? B) the 144,000 who were redeemed

📖 REVELATION 14:6–10

Pre-Quiz
1. Who had the everlasting gospel to preach to those still on the earth?
   A. a flying angel
   B. a golden ram
   C. a silver dove

2. An angel said that a great city had fallen. Which city?
   A. Old Jerusalem
   B. Babylon
   C. Egypt

3. Who was threatened to be tormented by fire and brimstone?

A. the Beast

B. anyone worshiping the Beast

C. the Dragon

What the Scriptures Say (Revelation 14:6–10)

Then I saw another angel flying in the midst of heaven, having the everlasting gospel to preach to those who dwell on the earth—to every nation, tribe, tongue, and people—saying with a loud voice, "Fear God and give glory to Him, for the hour of His judgment has come; and worship Him who made heaven and earth, the sea and springs of water."

And another angel followed, saying, "Babylon is fallen, is fallen, that great city, because she has made all nations drink of the wine of the wrath of her fornication."

Then a third angel followed them, saying with a loud voice, "If anyone worships the beast and his image, and receives his mark on his forehead or on his hand, he himself shall also drink of the wine of the wrath of God, which is poured out full strength into the cup of His indignation. He shall be tormented with fire and brimstone in the presence of the holy angels and in the presence of the Lamb."

What Revelation 14:6–10 Means

God uses four angels to help reveal His awareness of the suffering. In verse 6, we are introduced to the first angel. Directly in the midst of Satan's war on believers in Christ—a war in which Satan appears to be winning—God sends forth an angel to announce publicly to all the people who remain on earth that they can still be saved by having faith in Jesus' death and resurrection. Jesus must be accepted wholeheartedly. The angel will warn people to fear God instead of the Antichrist.

The second angel proclaims doom on Babylon. Babylon is the source of all false teachings regarding Christ and His kingdom, as we will learn in Revelation 17–18.

The third angel gives a dire warning about believing in the deceit and lies of Satan and the False Prophet. The angel also warns that judgment will fall upon those who receive the mark of the Beast.

Revelation 14:6–10 Quiz Answers
1. Who had the everlasting gospel to preach to those still on the earth? A) a flying angel
2. An angel said that a great city had fallen. Which city? B) Babylon
3. Who was threatened to be tormented by fire and brimstone? B) anyone worshiping the Beast

📖 REVELATION 14:11–13

Pre-Quiz
1. What remnant of torment goes up forever and ever?
   A. smoke
   B. incense
   C. fog

2. What attribute is identified in the saints who keep the commandments of God?
   A. love
   B. faith
   C. patience

3. Blessed are the dead who die in
   A. worship
   B. the Lord
   C. prayer

What the Scriptures Say (Revelation 14:11–13)
"And the smoke of their torment ascends forever and ever; and they have no rest day or night, who worship the beast and his image, and whoever

receives the mark of his name." Here is the patience of the saints; here are those who keep the commandments of God and the faith of Jesus.

Then I heard a voice from heaven saying to me, "Write: 'Blessed are the dead who die in the Lord from now on.' "

"Yes," says the Spirit, "that they may rest from their labors, and their works follow them."

What Revelation 14:11–13 Means

Scripture clearly states that those who worship the Beast and receive its mark will receive eternal torment. They will feel God's wrath forever without pause.

Those who die having made a commitment to follow the Lord are blessed.

Revelation 14:11–13 Quiz Answers

1. What remnant of torment goes up forever and ever? A) smoke
2. What attribute is attributed to the saints who keep the commandments of God? C) patience
3. Blessed are the dead who die in B) the Lord.

📖 REVELATION 14:14–20

Pre-Quiz

1. Who sat on the white cloud?
   A. the angels with harps
   B. Michael the archangel
   C. the Son of Man

2. He who was sitting on the cloud thrust what on the earth?
   A. his sword
   B. his sickle
   C. his staff

3. The angel that came out from the altar had authority over

   A. the sky

   B. water

   C. fire

What the Scriptures Say (Revelation 14:14–20)

Then I looked, and behold, a white cloud, and on the cloud sat One like the Son of Man, having on His head a golden crown, and in His hand a sharp sickle. And another angel came out of the temple, crying with a loud voice to Him who sat on the cloud, "Thrust in Your sickle and reap, for the time has come for You to reap, for the harvest of the earth is ripe." So He who sat on the cloud thrust in His sickle on the earth, and the earth was reaped.

Then another angel came out of the temple which is in heaven, he also having a sharp sickle. And another angel came out from the altar, who had power over fire, and he cried with a loud cry to him who had the sharp sickle, saying, "Thrust in your sharp sickle and gather the clusters of the vine of the earth, for her grapes are fully ripe." So the angel thrust his sickle into the earth and gathered the vine of the earth, and threw it into the great winepress of the wrath of God. And the winepress was trampled outside the city, and blood came out of the winepress, up to the horses' bridles, for one thousand six hundred furlongs.

What Revelation 14:14–20 Means

This is descriptive of the magnificent, glorified Jesus Christ in heaven before He descends to earth. This is just before He goes to war in the Battle of Armageddon. It's judgment for all those who have rejected Christ, despite innumerable opportunities to be a worshiper of the almighty God.

The "grapes are fully ripe" is the time period in which every living soul has chosen either Jesus or the Antichrist. There is no middle ground when the "grapes are fully ripe." This short period could be called the last chance to receive the Savior.

"Blood came out of the winepress" is symbolic of a mighty battle in which an enormous army will come against Christ in the Battle of Armageddon. Several early scriptures allude to this battle. Among them is Isaiah 63:1–4:

> Who is this who comes from Edom,
> With dyed garments from Bozrah,
> This One who is glorious in His apparel,
> Traveling in the greatness of His strength?—
> "I who speak in righteousness, mighty to save."
> Why is Your apparel red,
> And Your garments like one who treads in the winepress?
> "I have trodden the winepress alone,
> And from the peoples no one was with Me.
> For I have trodden them in My anger,
> And trampled them in My fury;
> Their blood is sprinkled upon My garments,
> And I have stained all My robes.
> For the day of vengeance is in My heart,
> And the year of My redeemed has come."

Jesus Christ, using the word of His mouth, will destroy the greatest collection of troops ever assembled in one location. Hailstones weighing approximately one hundred pounds each will fall from heaven with the blood of the rebellious army creating a river of blood that reaches up to horses' bridles, as we will learn in Revelation 16.

Revelation 14:14–20 Quiz Answers

1. Who sat on the white cloud? C) the Son of Man
2. He who was sitting on the cloud thrust what on the earth? B) his sickle
3. The angel that came out from the altar had authority over C) fire.

REVELATION

15

THE SEA OF GLASS

📖 **REVELATION 15:1–8**

Pre-Quiz

1. What was the great and marvelous sign John saw?
   - A. seven angels with seven plagues
   - B. the four elders on four horses
   - C. two angels, Michael and Gabriel

2. What did John see opened in heaven?
   - A. the lid of the golden chalice
   - B. the pearly gates
   - C. the temple of the tabernacle of the testimony

3. What was in the seven golden bowls given to the seven angels?
   - A. blood
   - B. the wrath of God
   - C. the tears of those in mourning

What the Scriptures Say (Revelation 15:1–8)

Then I saw another sign in heaven, great and marvelous: seven angels having the seven last plagues, for in them the wrath of God is complete. And I saw something like a sea of glass mingled with fire, and those who have the victory over the beast, over his image and over his mark and over the number of his name, standing on the sea of glass, having harps of God. They sing the song of Moses, the servant of God, and the song of the Lamb, saying:

"Great and marvelous are Your works,
  Lord God Almighty!
  Just and true are Your ways,
  O King of the saints!
  Who shall not fear You, O Lord, and glorify Your name?
  For You alone are holy.
  For all nations shall come and worship before You,
For Your judgments have been manifested."

After these things I looked, and behold, the temple of the tabernacle of the testimony in heaven was opened. And out of the temple came the seven angels having the seven plagues, clothed in pure bright linen, and having their chests girded with golden bands. Then one of the four living creatures gave to the seven angels seven golden bowls full of the wrath of God who lives forever and ever. The temple was filled with smoke from the glory of God and from His power, and no one was able to enter the temple till the seven plagues of the seven angels were completed.

What Revelation 15:1–8 Means

The shortest chapter in the book of Revelation, chapter 15 is an introduction to the Great Tribulation, which we will learn about in chapter 16.

In verse 1, John says he saw another great and marvelous sign. The key word is *another*. John is referring to the two previous signs of Revelation 12, one being the woman representing Israel and the other being the great red dragon representing Satan. This new, third sign is the most important of the three signs revealed to date.

Those who stand on the sea of glass have a significant victory. Killed by the Antichrist for refusing to bow down and worship his image, they are the souls of martyrs who died for God. Their victory lies in the fact that their persecution from Satan delivered them to heaven. They will stay in heaven and await the resurrection, which is in the last three and a half years of the Tribulation near the glorious appearing of the Son of God.

The song of Moses was sung after the victory over Pharaoh and his army that God provided for the children of Israel at the Red Sea. This is detailed in Exodus 15:1–3:

Then Moses and the children of Israel sang this song to the LORD, and spoke, saying:

"I will sing to the LORD,
> For He has triumphed gloriously!
> The horse and its rider
> He has thrown into the sea!
> The LORD is my strength and song,
> And He has become my salvation;
> He is my God, and I will praise Him;
> My father's God, and I will exalt Him.
> The LORD is a man of war;
The LORD is His name."

The martyrs joyfully reaffirm their trust in Christ with the Lamb's song. This song is very similar to the song the heavenly elders sang in Revelation 5:9: "And they sang a new song, saying: 'You are worthy to take the scroll, and to open its seals; for You were slain, and have redeemed us to God by Your blood out of every tribe and tongue and people and nation.'"

The seven golden bowls full of the wrath of God symbolize plagues that will be released upon the earth during the last three and a half years of the Tribulation. These plagues will severely punish the worshipers of the Antichrist.

The smoke of the glory of God fills the heavenly temple for the entirety of the remaining three and a half years. The smoke, or clout of God's glory, is previously profiled in Ezekiel 43:5: "The Spirit lifted me up and brought me into the inner court; and behold, the glory of the LORD filled the temple."

Revelation 15:1–8 Quiz Answers
1. What was the great and marvelous sign John saw? A) seven angels with seven plagues
2. What did John see opened in heaven? C) the temple of the tabernacle of the testimony
3. What was in the seven golden bowls given to the seven angels? B) the wrath of God

REVELATION

16

PREPARING FOR THE
SECOND COMING

📖 REVELATION 16:1–9

Pre-Quiz

1. When the first angel poured out his bowl upon the earth, what fell on the men who had the mark of the Beast?

   A. blindness

   B. a grievous sore

   C. pain and misery

2. When the second angel poured his bowl on the sea, what happened to every creature in the sea?

   A. They all died.

   B. They all came upon the land.

   C. They boiled in the burning waters.

3. What was the responsibility of the fourth angel?
   A. to create an oasis
   B. to burn men with fire
   C. to provide comfort for lost souls

What the Scriptures Say (Revelation 16:1–9)

Then I heard a loud voice from the temple saying to the seven angels, "Go and pour out the bowls of the wrath of God on the earth."

So the first went and poured out his bowl upon the earth, and a foul and loathsome sore came upon the men who had the mark of the beast and those who worshiped his image. Then the second angel poured out his bowl on the sea, and it became blood as of a dead man; and every living creature in the sea died. Then the third angel poured out his bowl on the rivers and springs of water, and they became blood. And I heard the angel of the waters saying:

"You are righteous, O Lord,
        The One who is and who was and who is to be,
        Because You have judged these things.
        For they have shed the blood of saints and prophets,
        And You have given them blood to drink.
For it is their just due."

And I heard another from the altar saying, "Even so, Lord God Almighty, true and righteous are Your judgments."

Then the fourth angel poured out his bowl on the sun, and power was given to him to scorch men with fire. And men were scorched with great heat, and they blasphemed the name of God who has power over these plagues; and they did not repent and give Him glory.

What Revelation 16:1–9 Means

Now we are firmly in the final seven judgments. These are the most powerful and most severe judgments of the Great Tribulation. This is a period in which the function is to prepare the world for the second coming of Christ. He will come in great power and glory.

The bowls represent plagues poured out by seven angels. They are not symbolic, but are literal plagues of catastrophic nature that will be poured out upon the earth. The first bowl is specifically for anyone who wears the mark of the Beast.

The "foul and loathsome sore" of verse 2 is very similar to the plague of boils that afflicted Egypt as described in Exodus 9. Because God has designated a specific group to receive this plague of boils, those with the mark of the Beast, we can be sure that He is shedding grace, mercy, and protection on His believers during this time, in the same way He had protected the Israelites during the plagues upon Egypt.

The bowl of the second angel is a plague upon the sea. The sea is turned to blood, making the waters uninhabitable. All marine life will die in the sea of blood.

We recall that God has already caused a third of the sea to turn to blood during the second trumpet. But this more devastating plague of the second bowl incorporates the entire sea and everything in it. The pollution and stench from dead marine life floating to the top of the waters not only will be unbearable to those on land but carries the potential for devastating disease. Worldwide shipping will cease to exist, causing unimaginable economic problems, and the plague will eliminate a vast supply of water.

In retaliation for the Antichrist's followers reveling in the blood of the saints, the third angel's bowl will turn the water in rivers and springs into blood. With the remaining sources of water tainted, the land will breed disease, despair, and pestilence. Without water, a basic necessity for life, the inhabitants of earth are now exceedingly desperate and riotous. This act by God is a vindication for all martyrs and an answer to the prayers of the souls under the altar as explained in Revelation 6.

The pouring out of the fourth angel's bowl brings an intense heat unlike anything the world has ever experienced. Despite the fact that a third of the sun will be darkened, the remaining two-thirds will be so intensely powerful and penetrative, that it will scorch and burn people with fire.

The combination of bloody waters and debilitating heat will be excruciating. The suffering will be immense; humankind will be going through a hellish experience.

All men will know this is God's work, but instead of taking the opportunity to repent, men will curse God with ghastly stubbornness.

Revelation 16:1–9 Quiz Answers

1. When the first angel poured out his bowl upon the earth, what fell on the men who had the mark of the Beast? B) a grievous sore
2. When the second angel poured his bowl on the sea, what happened to every creature in the sea? A) They all died.
3. What was the responsibility of the fourth angel? B) to burn men with fire

📖 REVELATION 16:10–17

Pre-Quiz

1. John saw three unclean spirits come out of the mouth of the
    A. highest volcano
    B. Euphrates River
    C. dragon

2. What type of spirits were working miracles?
    A. unclean spirits
    B. angels
    C. demons

3. When the seventh angel poured out his bowl into the air, a great voice said
    A. "It is done."
    B. "The end is near."
    C. "Repent before it is too late."

What the Scriptures Say (Revelation 16:10–17)

Then the fifth angel poured out his bowl on the throne of the beast, and his kingdom became full of darkness; and they gnawed their tongues because of the pain. They blasphemed the God of heaven because of their pains and their sores, and did not repent of their deeds. Then the sixth angel poured out his bowl on the great river Euphrates, and its water was dried up, so that the way of the kings from the east might be prepared. And I saw three unclean spirits like frogs coming out of the mouth of the dragon, out of the mouth of the beast, and out of the mouth of the false prophet. For they are spirits of demons, performing signs, which go out to the kings of the earth and of the whole world, to gather them to the battle of that great day of God Almighty.

"Behold, I am coming as a thief. Blessed is he who watches, and keeps his garments, lest he walk naked and they see his shame."

And they gathered them together to the place called in Hebrew, Armageddon.

Then the seventh angel poured out his bowl into the air, and a loud voice came out of the temple of heaven, from the throne, saying, "It is done!"

What Revelation 16:10–17 Means

The bowl of the fifth angel is specifically for the Beast and his kingdom. Immeasurable suffering will be heaped upon the followers of the Antichrist, and yet they still will not repent. God's only expression of mercy during the Tribulation period is the darkness He plunges upon the earth. The darkness comes directly after the intense, excruciating heat of the fourth bowl judgment, giving substantial relief from the fiery heat, but causing problems anew, as the Scriptures say, "they gnawed their tongues because of the pain." The darkness will initially cause relief, then exasperation, frustration, and terror. And yet, many will still curse God rather than repent and accept Him.

This judgment of darkness mimics the ninth plague of Egypt and is referenced previously in Amos 5:18: "Woe to you who desire the day of the LORD! For what good is the day of the LORD to you? It will be darkness, and not light."

And Nahum 1:6–8:

> Who can stand before His indignation?
> And who can endure the fierceness of His anger?
> His fury is poured out like fire,
> And the rocks are thrown down by Him.
> The LORD is good,
> A stronghold in the day of trouble;
> And He knows those who trust in Him.
> But with an overflowing flood
> He will make an utter end of its place,
> And darkness will pursue His enemies.

In verse 12, the sixth angel's bowl dries up the mighty river Euphrates. The river was in the eastern part of the old Roman Empire and for centuries had been a natural boundary between the East and the West. Without the waterway between them, the kings of the East and the West will join forces in the Battle of Armageddon.

The expression "Battle of Armageddon" is used to describe the definitive battle between the Antichrist and his forces of evil on the earth and Christ. Christ emerges triumphant as He will consume His enemies with the power of His mouth, as we will learn in chapter 19.

The united, hellish, satanic trinity of Satan, the Beast, and the False Prophet will send forth three unclean spirits like frogs "out of the mouth" of Satan. The agenda of the spirits will be to deceive the kings of the world into amassing armies to prepare for the Battle of Armageddon. The gathering place will be the Valley of Megiddo, which was once called the "ideal battlefield" by Napoleon.

When the seventh angel pours out his bowl into the air, the world experiences its most violent earthquake ever. The violence of the earthquake destroys the cities of the nations and is so devastating that John requires the next two chapters to describe it.

Revelation 16:10–17 Quiz Answers

1. John saw three unclean spirits come out of the mouth of the C) dragon.
2. What type of spirits were working miracles? C) demons
3. When the seventh angel poured out his bowl into the air, a great voice said A) "It is done."

📖 REVELATION 16:18–21

Pre-Quiz

1. What occurred, as has not been since men were on the earth?
   A. a flood
   B. a hurricane
   C. an earthquake

2. What rained down out of heaven on man?
   A. hail
   B. fire
   C. mercy

3. Which plague was called "exceedingly great"?
   A. frogs
   B. hail
   C. flies

What the Scriptures Say (Revelation 16:18–21)

And there were noises and thunderings and lightnings; and there was a great earthquake, such a mighty and great earthquake as had not occurred since men were on the earth. Now the great city was divided into three parts, and the cities of the nations fell. And great Babylon was remembered before God, to give her the cup of the wine of the fierceness of His wrath. Then every island fled away, and the mountains were not found. And great hail from heaven fell upon men, each hailstone about the weight of a talent. Men blasphemed God because of the plague of the hail, since that plague was exceedingly great.

What Revelation 16:18–21 Means

The mountains and islands of the world will be flattened, ravished by a catastrophic earthquake and pummeled by hailstones weighing up to one hundred pounds each. Men blasphemed God, blaming Him, not themselves, for the devastation and destruction caused by the hailstones. It is apparent to all that only God could produce a plague of this level.

Revelation 16:18–21 Quiz Answers

1. What occurred, as has not been since men were on the earth? C) an earthquake
2. What rained down out of heaven on man? A) hail
3. Which plague was called "exceedingly great"? B) hail

REVELATION

17

RIDING THE BEAST

📖 REVELATION 17:1–4

Pre-Quiz

1. John was shown the judgment of the great
   A. kings of the earth
   B. harlot
   C. dragon

2. When John was carried away into a desert, he saw a woman sitting on a scarlet-colored
   A. throne
   B. beast
   C. mountain

3. The woman holds a golden cup that was full of
   A. gold
   B. blood
   C. abominations

What the Scriptures Say (Revelation 17:1–4)

Then one of the seven angels who had the seven bowls came and talked with me, saying to me, "Come, I will show you the judgment of the great harlot who sits on many waters, with whom the kings of the earth committed fornication, and the inhabitants of the earth were made drunk with the wine of her fornication."

So he carried me away in the Spirit into the wilderness. And I saw a woman sitting on a scarlet beast which was full of names of blasphemy, having seven heads and ten horns. The woman was arrayed in purple and scarlet, and adorned with gold and precious stones and pearls, having in her hand a golden cup full of abominations and the filthiness of her fornication.

What Revelation 17:1–4 Means

The "scarlet beast" represents government. The "woman" represents religion. Both the beast/government and the woman/religion are directly opposed to Christ and His glorious kingdom.

There is a powerful universal system intact on earth as the great harlot (religion) has influence with political leaders of "many waters." The term "many waters" refers to "many nations."

In verse 3, the harlot is seen sitting on top of the scarlet beast (government), meaning she is in control of it. She will have tremendous power, and government is beneath her.

The seven heads are seven hills on which the woman sits, and we will learn that the seven "hills" are actually seven kings. There will be more information about this shortly, in Revelation 17:9.

You will also learn about the ten horns, which are ten additional kings, in Revelation 17:12.

Revelation 17:1–4 Quiz Answers

1. John was shown the judgment of the great B) harlot.
2. When John was carried away into a desert, he saw a woman sitting on a scarlet-colored B) beast.
3. The woman holds a golden cup that was full of C) abominations.

📖 REVELATION 17:5–10

Pre-Quiz

1. The woman John saw was drunk with the blood of the
   A. dragon
   B. sacrificial lamb
   C. saints

2. When they behold the Beast, what will those whose names were not written in the Book of Life do?
   A. run for the mountains
   B. marvel
   C. faint

3. Of the seven kings, how many have fallen?
   A. none
   B. three
   C. five

What the Scriptures Say (Revelation 17:5–10)

And on her forehead a name was written:

MYSTERY, BABYLON THE GREAT,
    THE MOTHER OF HARLOTS
    AND OF THE ABOMINATIONS
OF THE EARTH.

I saw the woman, drunk with the blood of the saints and with the blood of the martyrs of Jesus. And when I saw her, I marveled with great amazement.

But the angel said to me, "Why did you marvel? I will tell you the mystery of the woman and of the beast that carries her, which has the seven heads and the ten horns. The beast that you saw was, and is not, and will ascend out of the bottomless pit and go to perdition. And those who dwell on the earth will marvel, whose names are not written in the Book of Life from the foundation of the world, when they see the beast that was, and is not, and yet is. Here is the mind which has wisdom: The seven heads are seven mountains on which the woman sits. There are also seven kings. Five have fallen, one is, and the other has not yet come. And when he comes, he must continue a short time."

What Revelation 17:5–10 Means

In verse 5, "mother of harlots and of the abominations of the earth" refers to idolatry. The people of the earth are worshiping in an idolatrous religion, which is an abomination to God.

In the end times, the false religion will permeate the earth and convince many that it is authentic. This mass of unsaved humanity will be blasphemous and shun the true living God.

It was Jesus who said in John 18:36: "My kingdom is not of this world."

Verse 8 describes that the people of the time will be amazed when they see the Beast, because he once was, now is not, and yet will come. These people are unbelievers and always have been. They are described as people whose names have not been written in the Book of Life from the time of the creation of the world.

Another group cited are the saints who bore testimony to Jesus. As followers of Christ, they were killed by the sacrilegious religious system.

Revelation 17:5–10 Quiz Answers

1. The woman John saw was drunk with the blood of the C) saints.
2. When they behold the Beast, what will those whose names were not written in the Book of Life do? B) marvel
3. Of the seven kings, how many have fallen? C) five

📖 REVELATION 17:11–18

Pre-Quiz

1. What were the ten horns that John saw?
   A. ten kings
   B. ten plagues
   C. ten omens

2. The waters that John saw, where the harlot sits, are
   A. multitudes, nations, and tongues
   B. wars and rumors of wars
   C. the flood that will overtake man

3. The ten horns hate the harlot and make her
   A. suffer
   B. desolate and naked
   C. repent

What the Scriptures Say (Revelation 17:11–18)

"The beast that was, and is not, is himself also the eighth, and is of the seven, and is going to perdition. The ten horns which you saw are ten kings who have received no kingdom as yet, but they receive authority for one hour as kings with the beast. These are of one mind, and they will give their power and authority to the beast. These will make war with the Lamb, and the Lamb will overcome them, for He is Lord of lords and King of kings; and those who are with Him are called, chosen, and faithful."

Then he said to me, "The waters which you saw, where the harlot sits, are peoples, multitudes, nations, and tongues. And the ten horns which you saw on the beast, these will hate the harlot, make her desolate and naked, eat her flesh and burn her with fire. For God has put it into their hearts to fulfill His purpose, to be of one mind, and to give their kingdom to the beast, until the words of God are fulfilled. And the woman whom you saw is that great city which reigns over the kings of the earth."

What Revelation 17:11–18 Means

The ten horns are first mentioned in Daniel 7–8. They are leaders hand-picked by the Antichrist, whom he authorizes to govern the world. These ten leaders work together, united, and do the bidding of the Beast.

The leaders approve the killing of the faithful followers of Christ, and they will band together to fight against Jesus in the Battle of Armageddon. Followers who will join Christ in the battle are referred to as "called, chosen, and faithful."

The term "called, chosen, and faithful" has been used in other scriptures to describe God's true believers and followers. One such reference occurs in 1 Peter 2:9: "But you are a chosen generation, a royal priesthood, a holy nation, His own special people, that you may proclaim the praises of Him who called you out of darkness into His marvelous light."

The primary goal of the Antichrist is to destroy Jesus Christ. With Christ out of the way, the Antichrist would have free reign over the world, uninhibited and unconquerable. However, Jesus is the Lord of lords and the King of kings, and the Antichrist will be defeated, as it is written.

Verses 15–16 describe how the Beast, full of power from using his evil religious system, will turn against the harlot. The harlot was once arrayed in finery such as pearls and precious stones only to be devoured and destroyed in a horrific and graphic way. This type of backstabbing treachery is typical of the forces of evil. The harlot's destruction brings to mind Romans 6:23, which states that "the wages of sin is death."

An idolatrous worldwide religion engulfs the earth after the rapture of Christ's church. We learn that for the first half of the Tribulation, this false religion welds all traditional religions together and dominates politically. Yet, now in the midst of the Tribulation, the ten horns/kings under the function of the Beast will kill the harlot/religion, and the False Prophet will take over the leadership responsibilities. He will dictate the direction of all religious worship on the earth.

Revelation 17:11–18 Quiz Answers

1. What were the ten horns that John saw? A) ten kings
2. The waters that John saw, where the harlot sits, are A) multitudes, nations, and tongues.
3. The ten horns hate the harlot and make her B) desolate and naked.

REVELATION

18

JUDGMENT UPON BABYLON

📖 **REVELATION 18:1–10**

Pre-Quiz

1. When the angel cried that Babylon had fallen, what had Babylon become?
   A. a desert
   B. a dwelling place of demons
   C. solid rock

2. And John heard a voice saying not to be partakers of sin so that they may avoid
   A. the great earthquake
   B. plagues
   C. hell

3. How long did the judgment of Babylon take?

A. one hour

B. one day

C. one month

What the Scriptures Say (Revelation 18:1–10)

After these things I saw another angel coming down from heaven, having great authority, and the earth was illuminated with his glory. And he cried mightily with a loud voice, saying, "Babylon the great is fallen, is fallen, and has become a dwelling place of demons, a prison for every foul spirit, and a cage for every unclean and hated bird! For all the nations have drunk of the wine of the wrath of her fornication, the kings of the earth have committed fornication with her, and the merchants of the earth have become rich through the abundance of her luxury."

And I heard another voice from heaven saying, "Come out of her, my people, lest you share in her sins, and lest you receive of her plagues. For her sins have reached to heaven, and God has remembered her iniquities. Render to her just as she rendered to you, and repay her double according to her works; in the cup which she has mixed, mix double for her. In the measure that she glorified herself and lived luxuriously, in the same measure give her torment and sorrow; for she says in her heart, 'I sit as queen, and am no widow, and will not see sorrow.' Therefore her plagues will come in one day—death and mourning and famine. And she will be utterly burned with fire, for strong is the Lord God who judges her. The kings of the earth who committed fornication and lived luxuriously with her will weep and lament for her, when they see the smoke of her burning, standing at a distance for fear of her torment, saying, 'Alas, alas, that great city Babylon, that mighty city! For in one hour your judgment has come.' "

What Revelation 18:1–10 Means

After reading verses 1–2 of Revelation 18, a logical question arises: if Babylon was destroyed in chapter 17, how does it reappear in chapter 18?

Chapter 17 refers symbolically to the religious Babylon, while chapter

18 refers to the commercial and political systems of Babylon. Chapter 18 describes destruction that will rid the world of devastating evils that have plagued mankind for thousands of years. We have just gone through the destruction of the religious Babylon in the middle of the Tribulation. The final destruction of the commercial and government Babylon systems will occur later, at the end of the Tribulation period.

These prophecies that show that the three end-time forces—economy, religion, and government—will all be destroyed at the same time in Babylon have many scholars believing that Babylon will be rebuilt by the Antichrist in the old city of Babylon, and used as his international capital of the world.

It will, of course, be his citadel of evil that he will run by technology in his last-ditch attempt to dethrone God and His Son, Jesus. He will fail.

Here is what Isaiah 13:19–22 says about Babylon:

> And Babylon, the glory of kingdoms,
> The beauty of the Chaldeans' pride,
> Will be as when God overthrew Sodom and Gomorrah.
> It will never be inhabited,
> Nor will it be settled from generation to generation;
> Nor will the Arabian pitch tents there,
> Nor will the shepherds make their sheepfolds there.
> But wild beasts of the desert will lie there,
> And their houses will be full of owls;
> Ostriches will dwell there,
> And wild goats will caper there.
> The hyenas will howl in their citadels,
> And jackals in their pleasant palaces.
> Her time is near to come,
> And her days will not be prolonged.

Historically this has not yet happened but is scheduled to be one of the last events of the Tribulation. The commercial and governmental systems represented by this Babylon will be abolished at the end of the Tribulation.

Verse 3 tells us that "all nations have drunk of the wine of the wrath of her fornication," meaning that every nation interacts with Babylon and is affected in some way by such interactions. The tentacles of Babylon will reach around the world.

In verse 4, the Lord is still saving souls, as a large multitude of people will finally realize that He truly is the Lord Almighty and that the gospel message of Jesus Christ can save them. The call from heaven warns these young believers to leave Babylon before it is destroyed. Heaven's response is to rejoice that the martyrs' and prophets' deaths are avenged.

In verses 5–8, the Lord has not overlooked, nor has He forgotten about, the wickedness of the earth's powerful, who for centuries use commerce and government to live well above others. These systems of the Antichrist—social, commercial, and political—will receive twice the judgment for their sin and wickedness.

The kings of the earth, not wanting to feel the wrath that is poured out on Babylon, will stand "at a distance," at what they feel is a safe ways away.

Revelation 18:1–10 Quiz Answers

1. When the angel cried that Babylon had fallen, what had Babylon become? B) a dwelling place of demons
2. John heard a voice saying not to be partakers of sin so that they may avoid B) plagues.
3. How long did the judgment of Babylon take? A) one hour

📖 REVELATION 18:11–19

Pre-Quiz

1. According to Revelation 18:14, what would you find no more?
   A. salvation
   B. mercy
   C. fruits of the lust of your soul

2. What had the great city been clothed in?

   A. animal fur

   B. fine linen and purple

   C. gold

3. What did those who were weeping and mourning throw on their heads?

   A. dust

   B. saltwater

   C. frankincense

What the Scriptures Say (Revelation 18:11–19)

"And the merchants of the earth will weep and mourn over her, for no one buys their merchandise anymore: merchandise of gold and silver, precious stones and pearls, fine linen and purple, silk and scarlet, every kind of citron wood, every kind of object of ivory, every kind of object of most precious wood, bronze, iron, and marble; and cinnamon and incense, fragrant oil and frankincense, wine and oil, fine flour and wheat, cattle and sheep, horses and chariots, and bodies and souls of men. The fruit that your soul longed for has gone from you, and all the things which are rich and splendid have gone from you, and you shall find them no more at all. The merchants of these things, who became rich by her, will stand at a distance for fear of her torment, weeping and wailing, and saying, 'Alas, alas, that great city that was clothed in fine linen, purple, and scarlet, and adorned with gold and precious stones and pearls! For in one hour such great riches came to nothing.' Every shipmaster, all who travel by ship, sailors, and as many as trade on the sea, stood at a distance and cried out when they saw the smoke of her burning, saying, 'What is like this great city?' They threw dust on their heads and cried out, weeping and wailing, and saying, 'Alas, alas, that great city, in which all who had ships on the sea became rich by her wealth! For in one hour she is made desolate.'"

What Revelation 18:11–19 Means

Merchants of the earth are not mourning human loss, but rather are ruing the loss of business and income. Jewelry merchants who peddle gold, silver, precious metals, pearls, and other gems will mourn. Clothing merchants who sold fine linen, purple silk, and scarlet-colored garments will grieve and lament their losses. Merchants of fine furniture made of various combinations of wood, ivory, brass, iron, and marble will bemoan the loss of business.

Cosmetics merchants will mourn the loss of sales of cinnamon, ointments, and frankincense. Food merchants who peddled wine, oil, fine flour, and various meats will mourn the loss of sales. Merchants of transportation, such as those who sold horses and chariots, will mourn the loss of business. Those in the prostitution and slave business, the marketing of humans, will feel a devastating loss of revenue. The economical effect is demoralizing as merchants have no one to sell their wares to.

The types of things sold in Babylon give us a glimpse into what was valued most. All the wares mentioned, except for food, are luxury items, not necessities and certainly not our daily bread.

The destruction of Babylon brings about two opposite responses. The people's response is to weep and wail. Heaven's response is to rejoice.

Revelation 18:11–19 Quiz Answers

1. According to Revelation 18:14, what would you find no more? C) fruits of the lust of your soul
2. What had the great city been clothed in? B) fine linen and purple
3. What did those who were weeping and mourning throw on their heads? A) dust

📖 REVELATION 18:20–24

Pre-Quiz

1. What did one strong angel throw into the sea?
   A. the moon
   B. the sun
   C. a millstone

2. Revelation 18:23 states that which type of light will never shine in [Babylon] again?
   A. the light of the sun
   B. the light of a lamp
   C. the light of God

3. By what were all nations deceived?
   A. sorceries
   B. false prophets
   C. misguided hope

What the Scriptures Say (Revelation 18:20–24)

"Rejoice over her, O heaven, and you holy apostles and prophets, for God has avenged you on her!"

Then a mighty angel took up a stone like a great millstone and threw it into the sea, saying, "Thus with violence the great city Babylon shall be thrown down, and shall not be found anymore. The sound of harpists, musicians, flutists, and trumpeters shall not be heard in you anymore. No craftsman of any craft shall be found in you anymore, and the sound of a millstone shall not be heard in you anymore. The light of a lamp shall not shine in you anymore, and the voice of bridegroom and bride shall not be heard in you anymore. For your merchants were the great men of the earth, for by your sorcery all the nations were deceived. And in her was found the blood of prophets and saints, and of all who were slain on the earth."

What Revelation 18:20–24 Means

"Sorcery" describes the widespread use of illicit drugs and the practice and worship of the occult, which was prevalent at this time.

The angel casting a millstone into the sea is representative of how the Antichrist's kingdom will be completely and thoroughly destroyed. It is also an indictment of those who lived solely for pleasure and material things.

Revelation 18:20–24 Quiz Answers

1. What did one strong angel throw into the sea? C) a millstone
2. Revelation 18:23 states that which type of light will never shine in [Babylon] again? B) the light of a lamp
3. By what were all nations deceived? A) sorceries

REVELATION

19

CHRIST RETURNS

📖 **REVELATION 19:1–10**

Pre-Quiz

1. Who said alleluia?
    A. a great multitude in heaven
    B. the angels around the throne
    C. the remaining people of earth

2. The marriage of what has come?
    A. the Beast to the dragon
    B. the bride to the Bridegroom
    C. the Lamb

3. The testimony of Jesus is the spirit of
    A. prophecy
    B. signs and wonders
    C. joy and mourning

What the Scriptures Say (Revelation 19:1–10)

After these things I heard a loud voice of a great multitude in heaven, saying, "Alleluia! Salvation and glory and honor and power belong to the Lord our God! For true and righteous are His judgments, because He has judged the great harlot who corrupted the earth with her fornication; and He has avenged on her the blood of His servants shed by her."

Again they said, "Alleluia! Her smoke rises up forever and ever!"

And the twenty-four elders and the four living creatures fell down and worshiped God who sat on the throne, saying, "Amen! Alleluia!"

Then a voice came from the throne, saying, "Praise our God, all you His servants and those who fear Him, both small and great!"

And I heard, as it were, the voice of a great multitude, as the sound of many waters and as the sound of mighty thunderings, saying, "Alleluia! For the Lord God Omnipotent reigns! Let us be glad and rejoice and give Him glory, for the marriage of the Lamb has come, and His wife has made herself ready." And to her it was granted to be arrayed in fine linen, clean and bright, for the fine linen is the righteous acts of the saints.

Then he said to me, "Write: 'Blessed are those who are called to the marriage supper of the Lamb!'" And he said to me, "These are the true sayings of God." And I fell at his feet to worship him. But he said to me, "See that you do not do that! I am your fellow servant, and of your brethren who have the testimony of Jesus. Worship God! For the testimony of Jesus is the spirit of prophecy."

What Revelation 19:1–10 Means

Revelation 19 is triumphant and celebrated. It begins after the complete destruction of Babylon, the political and commercial center at the heart of an evil, wicked world. Yet, while the people on earth suffered, those in heaven continued to rejoice.

The church, which is the bride of Christ, is the honored guest at the marriage of the Lamb. This takes place in heaven, and the church joins Christ in His second coming. It is a time of triumph and delight.

Revelation 19 is the only place in the New Testament that includes the word *alleluia*, which appears four times. *Alleluia* means "praise the Lord." Along with the word *amen*, they are the only two words in existence that are known in every single language on earth.

People in heaven are celebratory and are singing about salvation. All Christ's faithful believers, including those from the Old Testament times, are joined together in a magnificent chorus of "Alleluia."

Because the marriage of the Lamb and the marriage supper of the Lamb are in heaven, we can be assured that the church is already established in heaven before Christ returns to earth. The Bridegroom is Christ, and His bride is the church. Since the word *church* or *churches* appears nineteen times in the first three chapters of Revelation, and not again until Revelation 22:16, we can conclude that the church (Christ's faithful) was not on earth during the judgments of Revelation in chapters 4 through 18.

Verse 10 mentions prophecy. Many things concerning Jesus are prophetic, including His birth, which involves 109 prophecies, His life on earth, His death and resurrection, and, of course, His second coming.

Revelation 19:1–10 Quiz Answers
1. Who said alleluia? A) a great multitude in heaven
2. The marriage of what has come? C) the Lamb
3. The testimony of Jesus is the spirit of A) prophecy.

📖 REVELATION 19:11–13

Pre-Quiz
1. In Revelation 19:11, when heaven opened, what was beheld?
   A. God Himself
   B. a white horse
   C. the judgment of God

2. What was the name of the rider of the white horse?
   A. Fiery Judgment
   B. Truth and Righteousness
   C. Faithful and True

3. The rider of the white horse was wearing a garment dipped in
   A. blood
   B. melted gold
   C. truth

What the Scriptures Say (Revelation 19:11–13)

Now I saw heaven opened, and behold, a white horse. And He who sat on him was called Faithful and True, and in righteousness He judges and makes war. His eyes were like a flame of fire, and on His head were many crowns. He had a name written that no one knew except Himself. He was clothed with a robe dipped in blood, and His name is called The Word of God.

What Revelation 19:11–13 Means

The door to heaven is opened. In Revelation 4:1, the door to heaven is opened for the raptured church. Now, seven years later, it is opened again.

Heroically, here comes Jesus Christ, prepared for war against the kings of the earth, Satan, the Antichrist, and the False Prophet. Jesus rides a white horse and has "many crowns" on His head. When He is finished with Satan, Jesus becomes the master and absolute ruler of the earth.

Revelation 19:11–13 Quiz Answers

1. In Revelation 19:11, when heaven opened, what was beheld? B) a white horse
2. What was the name of the rider of the white horse? C) Faithful and True
3. The rider of the white horse was wearing a garment dipped in A) blood.

📖 REVELATION 19:14–18

Pre-Quiz

1. Out of Jesus' mouth goes a sharp sword to strike the
    A. waters
    B. nations
    C. mountains

2. What name is written on His thigh?
    A. Jesus
    B. King of the Jews
    C. King of kings and Lord of lords

3. An angel cried to the birds calling them to eat the flesh of
    A. kings
    B. crows
    C. demons

What the Scriptures Say (Revelation 19:14–18)

And the armies in heaven, clothed in fine linen, white and clean, followed Him on white horses. Now out of His mouth goes a sharp sword, that with it He should strike the nations. And He Himself will rule them with a rod of iron. He Himself treads the winepress of the fierceness and wrath of Almighty God. And He has on His robe and on His thigh a name written:

KING OF KINGS AND
LORD OF LORDS.

Then I saw an angel standing in the sun; and he cried with a loud voice, saying to all the birds that fly in the midst of heaven, "Come and gather together for the supper of the great God, that you may eat the flesh of kings, the flesh of captains, the flesh of mighty men, the flesh of horses and of those who sit on them, and the flesh of all people, free and slave, both small and great."

What Revelation 19:14–18 Means

With the door in heaven open, the Lord's faithful are clothed in white linen. The faithful are not there to engage in the battle but to observe Jesus in victory.

The "sharp sword" that comes forth from the mouth of Jesus is not a literal sword. It is the Word He speaks that is sharper than any two-edged sword, as mentioned in Hebrews 4:12: "For the word of God is living and powerful, and sharper than any two-edged sword, piercing even to the division of soul and spirit, and of joints and marrow, and is a discerner of the thoughts and intents of the heart."

Jesus conquers without earthly weapons such as tanks and missiles. He conquers with the Word.

"KING OF KINGS AND LORD OF LORDS" is the name written on Jesus' thigh, meaning He and He alone is above all things whether natural or supernatural. Only He can have such a title as He returns to set up His millennial kingdom (one thousand years) upon the earth.

In the Old Testament, Isaiah 65:17–25 gives very descriptive details about the Millennium. This helps to prove that Jerusalem, a place that has been subjected to much terror throughout its history, will become a place of rejoicing, with no more weeping. It reads:

> "For behold, I create new heavens and a new earth;
> And the former shall not be remembered or come to mind.
> But be glad and rejoice forever in what I create;
> For behold, I create Jerusalem as a rejoicing,
> And her people a joy.
> I will rejoice in Jerusalem,
> And joy in My people;

The voice of weeping shall no longer be heard in her,
Nor the voice of crying.

"No more shall an infant from there live but a few days,
Nor an old man who has not fulfilled his days;
For the child shall die one hundred years old,
But the sinner being one hundred years old shall be accursed.
They shall build houses and inhabit them;
They shall plant vineyards and eat their fruit.
They shall not build and another inhabit;
They shall not plant and another eat;
For as the days of a tree, so shall be the days of My people,
And My elect shall long enjoy the work of their hands.
They shall not labor in vain,
Nor bring forth children for trouble;
For they shall be the descendants of the blessed of the LORD,
And their offspring with them.

"It shall come to pass
That before they call, I will answer;
And while they are still speaking, I will hear.
The wolf and the lamb shall feed together,
The lion shall eat straw like the ox,
And dust shall be the serpent's food.
They shall not hurt nor destroy in all My holy mountain,"
Says the LORD.

Revelation 19:14–18 Quiz Answers
1. Out of Jesus' mouth goes a sharp sword to strike the B) nations.
2. What name is written on His thigh? C) King of kings and Lord of lords
3. An angel cried to the birds calling them to eat the flesh of A) kings.

📖 REVELATION 19:19–21

Pre-Quiz

    1. What was seen with the Beast and the kings of the earth?

        A. demons

        B. fallen angels

        C. their armies

    2. Who was thrown alive into the lake of fire?

        A. the false prophets

        B. the Beast and the False Prophet

        C. unbelievers

    3. What happened to the rest?

        A. They were slain by the sword.

        B. They were captured by the dragon.

        C. They were swallowed by birds.

What the Scriptures Say (Revelation 19:19–21)

And I saw the beast, the kings of the earth, and their armies, gathered together to make war against Him who sat on the horse and against His army. Then the beast was captured, and with him the false prophet who worked signs in his presence, by which he deceived those who received the mark of the beast and those who worshiped his image. These two were cast alive into the lake of fire burning with brimstone. And the rest were killed with the sword which proceeded from the mouth of Him who sat on the horse. And all the birds were filled with their flesh.

What Revelation 19:19–21 Means

The Beast and the False Prophet are vanquished by Jesus. They had been pawns of Satan, used to trick men and keep them from believing in God during the Tribulation. Jesus will hurl them "alive into the lake of fire."

This horrific lake is actually an eternal hell that, according to Matthew 25:41, was prepared for the devil and his angels.

When Satan is cast into the lake of fire one thousand years later, the Beast and the False Prophet are still there in captivity. This is further indication that their punishment is eternal.

In the final verse of Revelation 19, Jesus Christ destroys all that had campaigned and blasphemed against Him. The bodies He leaves on earth become food for birds.

The souls of those who rebelled against God will go to the place of torment, where the souls will await the Great White Throne Judgment after the Millennium.

Revelation 19:19–21 Quiz Answers

1. What was seen with the Beast and the kings of the earth? C) their armies
2. Who was thrown alive into the lake of fire? B) the Beast and the False Prophet
3. What happened to the rest? A) They were slain by the sword.

REVELATION

SATAN IS BOUND

📖 REVELATION 20:1–4

Pre-Quiz

1. Who is that old serpent?
   A. Magog
   B. Babylon
   C. Satan

2. How long will Satan be bound?
   A. forty days and forty nights
   B. seven years
   C. one thousand years

3. John saw the souls of those who suffered for the witness of Jesus.
   They had been
   A. beheaded
   B. crucified
   C. stoned

What the Scriptures Say (Revelation 20:1–4)

Then I saw an angel coming down from heaven, having the key to the bottomless pit and a great chain in his hand. He laid hold of the dragon, that serpent of old, who is the Devil and Satan, and bound him for a thousand years; and he cast him into the bottomless pit, and shut him up, and set a seal on him, so that he should deceive the nations no more till the thousand years were finished. But after these things he must be released for a little while. And I saw thrones, and they sat on them, and judgment was committed to them. Then I saw the souls of those who had been beheaded for their witness to Jesus and for the word of God, who had not worshiped the beast or his image, and had not received his mark on their foreheads or on their hands. And they lived and reigned with Christ for a thousand years.

What Revelation 20:1–4 Means

Christ's millennial kingdom begins. Satan is captured, bound, and imprisoned in the bottomless pit for one thousand years. Christ uses an angel to manhandle and imprison Satan.

The length of time chosen, one thousand years, is a real and exact time. During this time, with the complete absence of Satan, a new utopia is formed on the earth. With no Satan to further deceive man, Christ will reign alone and supremely.

The fact that Christ uses a single angel to incapacitate Satan displays Christ's immeasurable power in comparison to Satan's. It also proves that Satan is not the complete opposite of God, an equally powerful, but evil version. God and Satan are not, nor have they ever been, equals, with one being good and the other evil. God has no equal, and Satan is no match whatsoever for the power of the Lord.

Remember, according to Matthew 26:63–66, it was Satan behind the high priests' plot to have Jesus placed in a tomb:

And the high priest answered and said to Him, "I put You under oath by the living God: Tell us if You are the Christ, the Son of God!"

Jesus said to him, "It is as you said. Nevertheless, I say to you, hereafter you will see the Son of Man sitting at the right hand of the Power, and coming on the clouds of heaven."

Then the high priest tore his clothes, saying, "He has spoken blasphemy! What further need do we have of witnesses? Look, now you have heard His blasphemy! What do you think?"

They answered and said, "He is deserving of death."

Of course, Jesus emerged triumphantly, three days and nights later exactly as He promised. Now with the tables turned, Satan will not be able to escape the fate that Christ has selected for him.

Verse 4 mentions those who had been beheaded for their faithfulness to Christ. Back in Revelation 6:9–11, we learned that many will be slain by the Antichrist during the Tribulation for failure to receive his mark. Revelation 20:4 completes the circle in which the beheaded faithful will be resurrected to reign with Christ during His one-thousand-year kingdom upon the earth.

Revelation 20:1–4 Quiz Answers
1. Who is that old serpent? C) Satan
2. How long will Satan be bound? C) one thousand years
3. John saw the souls of those who suffered for the witness of Jesus. They had been A) beheaded.

📖 REVELATION 20:5–10

Pre-Quiz
1. The rest of the dead did not live again until
   A. all who were alive died
   B. one thousand years had passed
   C. the seventh seal was opened

2. What happens after the thousand years have expired?

   A. There will be peace for another thousand years.

   B. Satan will be loosed.

   C. A new earth will replace the old earth.

3. Who will be tormented day and night forever and ever?

   A. the kings of the earth

   B. the devil

   C. the harlot

What the Scriptures Say (Revelation 20:5–10)

But the rest of the dead did not live again until the thousand years were finished. This is the first resurrection. Blessed and holy is he who has part in the first resurrection. Over such the second death has no power, but they shall be priests of God and of Christ, and shall reign with Him a thousand years. Now when the thousand years have expired, Satan will be released from his prison and will go out to deceive the nations which are in the four corners of the earth, Gog and Magog, to gather them together to battle, whose number is as the sand of the sea. They went up on the breadth of the earth and surrounded the camp of the saints and the beloved city. And fire came down from God out of heaven and devoured them. The devil, who deceived them, was cast into the lake of fire and brimstone where the beast and the false prophet are. And they will be tormented day and night forever and ever.

What Revelation 20:5–10 Means

The "first resurrection" is for the faithful of Christ, but takes place in sections. The first part is listed in 1 Corinthians 15:20, with Christ as the firstfruits: "But now Christ is risen from the dead, and has become the firstfruits of those who have fallen asleep."

The next part of the "first resurrection" is the rapture of the church. First Corinthians 15:23 says: "But each one in his own order: Christ the firstfruits, afterward those who are Christ's at His coming." First Thessalonians 4:13–18 also discusses the death of believers:

But I do not want you to be ignorant, brethren, concerning those who have fallen asleep, lest you sorrow as others who have no hope. For if we believe that Jesus died and rose again, even so God will bring with Him those who sleep in Jesus.

For this we say to you by the word of the Lord, that we who are alive and remain until the coming of the Lord will by no means precede those who are asleep. For the Lord Himself will descend from heaven with a shout, with the voice of an archangel, and with the trumpet of God. And the dead in Christ will rise first. Then we who are alive and remain shall be caught up together with them in the clouds to meet the Lord in the air. And thus we shall always be with the Lord. Therefore comfort one another with these words.

Thus, the Tribulation saints are raised up along with the Old Testament saints. This is first mentioned in Psalm 50:1–6:

> The Mighty One, God the LORD,
> Has spoken and called the earth
> From the rising of the sun to its going down.
> Out of Zion, the perfection of beauty,
> God will shine forth.
> Our God shall come, and shall not keep silent;
> A fire shall devour before Him,
> And it shall be very tempestuous all around Him.
>
> He shall call to the heavens from above,
> And to the earth, that He may judge His people:
> "Gather My saints together to Me,
> Those who have made a covenant with Me by sacrifice."
> Let the heavens declare His righteousness,
> For God Himself is Judge.

The "first resurrection" includes everyone who believes in Christ up to the period in which Christ returns to the earth. The second resurrection is exclusively for all those who did not believe. The "second death" is final. It involves entry into the lake of fire for all those who have rejected the Lord, as we will learn in Revelation 21:8.

We cannot help but grieve for those lost souls who have had many opportunities to submit their free will to God in the name of His Son, Jesus, but they willed, by free choice, not to come to Him. As tragic as their eternal destiny is, after many opportunities to be saved, they rebelled at God's offer of salvation by faith.

Gog and Magog have been mentioned before in Ezekiel 38. Yet, these are not the same version. Now, after one thousand years, Satan is released from imprisonment.

Verse 8 refers to the population of the world. "As the sand of the sea" indicates a tremendous population at the end of the Millennium. Astonishingly, there are still hearts that rebel against Jesus Christ. Jeremiah 17:9 states: "The heart is deceitful above all things, and desperately wicked; who can know it?"

In verse 9, the beloved city is the millennial version of Jerusalem. It is exasperating and unbelievable that humans could and would live under the spectacularly righteous reign of Jesus for one thousand years and then follow Satan as soon as Satan is released. It is a testimony to Satan's deceitful tactics and man's gullibility. Thus, God sends fire down from heaven that devours Satan and all his followers.

Satan receives his final fate along with all his followers and all unbelievers. They are all cast into the lake of fire. For a human being, the lake of fire is unimaginably horrid, as it was not designed for man, but for Satan and his fallen angels. Matthew 25:41 states: "Then He will also say to those on the left hand, 'Depart from Me, you cursed, into the everlasting fire prepared for the devil and his angels.'"

Entry into the lake of fire is called the "second death," because there is no escape and no possibility for release for all eternity.

Revelation 20:5–10 Quiz Answers

1. The rest of the dead did not live again until B) one thousand years had passed.

2. What happens after the thousand years have expired? B) Satan will be loosed.

3. Who will be tormented day and night forever and ever? B) the devil

📖 REVELATION 20:11–15

Pre-Quiz

1. Who did John see standing before God?

    A. the lost

    B. the consumed

    C. the dead

2. And the dead were judged out of the things written in

    A. blood

    B. the books according to their works

    C. the ancient scrolls

3. What was now cast into the lake of fire?

    A. the red dragon

    B. Death and Hades

    C. the condemned

What the Scriptures Say (Revelation 20:11–15)

Then I saw a great white throne and Him who sat on it, from whose face the earth and the heaven fled away. And there was found no place for them. And I saw the dead, small and great, standing before God, and books were opened. And another book was opened, which is the Book of Life. And the dead were judged according to their works, by the things which were written in the books. The sea gave up the dead who were in it, and Death and Hades delivered up the dead who were in them. And they were judged, each one according to his works. Then Death and Hades were cast into the lake of fire. This is the second death.

And anyone not found written in the Book of Life was cast into the lake of fire.

What Revelation 20:11–15 Means

At the conclusion of the Millennium, those who refused to accept Jesus Christ as their Lord and Savior must stand before God. The "dead" are those who are spiritually dead because of this rejection. In a resurrected form, they will stand before Christ Himself to be judged. John 5:22 says, "For the Father judges no one, but has committed all judgment to the Son."

Books (scrolls) are opened in verse 12. The dead are all who have been in hell, which is a temporary holding place for the souls of the faithless until their judgment day arrives. All the way back from the book of Genesis and Cain, through to the final unsuccessful rebellion, all who did not believe in Christ are there. Only unbelievers are at this judgment.

There is no escaping God's final judgment. The unbelievers will be taken out from the sea and graves in a massive resurrection, only to be judged and cast into the lake of fire.

And with one final act of mercy, God reviews the Book of Life in search of the names of any of these unbelievers at the final judgment.

None will be found. For even though their names had been written in anticipation of their being saved, their rejection during life, upon their deaths will cause their names to be "blotted out." Psalms 9:5 reads, "You have rebuked the nations, You have destroyed the wicked; You have blotted out their name forever and ever."

This is one final evidence that "the Lord is not . . . willing that any should perish but that all should come to repentance" (2 Peter 3:9). What a tragedy they refuse to do so!

Revelation 20:11–15 Quiz Answers

1. Who did John see standing before God? C) the dead
2. And the dead were judged out of the things written in B) the books according to their works.
3. What was now cast into the lake of fire? B) Death and Hades

REVELATION

21

THE NEW HEAVEN AND THE NEW EARTH

The final two chapters of Revelation will reveal seven new things. These things allow a glimpse into the future that God has prepared for all those who love Him and have been faithful.

- a new heaven (21:1)
- a new earth (21:1)
- New Jerusalem (21:2)
- new things (21:5)
- a new paradise (22:1–5)
- a new place for God's throne (22:3)
- a new source of light (22:5)

📖 REVELATION 21:1–8

Pre-Quiz

1. What was the name of the holy city John saw?
   A. New Babylon
   B. New Jerusalem
   C. New Jordan

2. John was told to resume
   A. writing
   B. praying
   C. repenting

3. Where will the unbelieving, the abominable, murderers, the sexually immoral, sorcerers, and idolaters be placed?
   A. hell
   B. Hades
   C. lake burning with fire and brimstone

What the Scriptures Say (Revelation 21:1–8)

Now I saw a new heaven and a new earth, for the first heaven and the first earth had passed away. Also there was no more sea. Then I, John, saw the holy city, New Jerusalem, coming down out of heaven from God, prepared as a bride adorned for her husband. And I heard a loud voice from heaven saying, "Behold, the tabernacle of God is with men, and He will dwell with them, and they shall be His people. God Himself will be with them and be their God. And God will wipe away every tear from their eyes; there shall be no more death, nor sorrow, nor crying. There shall be no more pain, for the former things have passed away."

Then He who sat on the throne said, "Behold, I make all things new." And He said to me, "Write, for these words are true and faithful."

And He said to me, "It is done! I am the Alpha and the Omega, the Beginning and the End. I will give of the fountain of the water of life freely to him who thirsts. He who overcomes shall inherit all things, and I will be his God and he shall be My son. But the cowardly, unbelieving, abominable, murderers, sexually immoral, sorcerers, idolaters, and all liars shall have their part in the lake which burns with fire and brimstone, which is the second death."

What Revelation 21:1–8 Means

Revelation 21 introduces us to a "new heaven." This is an area above and around the earth that had been Satan's domain, as stated in Ephesians 2:2: "in which you once walked according to the course of this world, according to the prince of the power of the air, the spirit who now works in the sons of disobedience."

It is a "new" heaven because it must be cleansed. It needs to be unadulterated and pure before the Lord comes down to the new earth. The aura of filth and pollution left behind by Satan will be completely eliminated.

The new earth is utopia, similar to the garden of Eden in its original form. An interesting and amazing aspect of the new earth will be the lack of the vast oceans that cover more than 70 percent of our present world. There will be much more land that is fully inhabitable, lush, and idyllic for God's redeemed followers.

Christ has been building mansions, not houses or homes, but mansions, for His bride, which is his faithful church of followers and believers. This fact is mentioned in John 14:1–4: "Let not your heart be troubled; you believe in God, believe also in Me. In My Father's house are many mansions; if it were not so, I would have told you. I go to prepare a place for you. And if I go and prepare a place for you, I will come again and receive you to Myself; that where I am, there you may be also. And where I go you know, and the way you know."

God's prophetic commands dictate that after the Millennium, Christ will bring the new holy city, New Jerusalem, to the new, beautified, glorified earth. This is where Christ will have His capital city for all eternity. This magnificent city is prepared as a wedding gift for the bride of Jesus Christ, His worshipers.

The tabernacle is literal and implies God will dwell among His people. This is coming to fruition as verse 3 states that God will dwell with man. This is an eternal state lasting forever, in which the redeemed and faithful followers will have fellowship not only with their loved ones but also with God Himself.

No tears, pain, sorrow, or death will be present in the New Jerusalem where Christ's followers will live. This reverses forever the curse that came from Adam's sin in Genesis 3:16–19:

> To the woman He said:
> "I will greatly multiply your sorrow and your conception;
>> In pain you shall bring forth children;
>> Your desire shall be for your husband,
>> And he shall rule over you."

> Then to Adam He said, "Because you have heeded the voice of your wife, and have eaten from the tree of which I commanded you, saying, 'You shall not eat of it':

> "Cursed is the ground for your sake;
>> In toil you shall eat of it
>> All the days of your life.
>> Both thorns and thistles it shall bring forth for you,
>> And you shall eat the herb of the field.
>> In the sweat of your face you shall eat bread
>> Till you return to the ground,
>> For out of it you were taken;
>> For dust you are,
>> And to dust you shall return."

Adam's curse is no more. Creation is not merely fixed; it is reconstructed for God's children to revel in for all eternity.

"It is done!" With utter finality, God's promise to His saints has been fulfilled.

As the bride of Christ, the faithful followers of Jesus inherit all that He has, as He has promised that He will be our God, and we will be His son.

Yet, as the followers of Christ enjoy heavenly bliss on earth, Revelation 21 graphically outlines the trials and tribulations of the horrible fate of nonbelievers of all sorts, who will experience the "second death." The Lord calls out unbelievers by their offenses: murderers, the sexually immoral, sorcerers, idolaters, and all liars. He will have them placed in the lake of fire because of their stubbornness, ignorance, unbelief, and continual sin.

Revelation 21:1–8 Quiz Answers

1. What was the name of the holy city John saw? B) New Jerusalem
2. John was told to resume A) writing.
3. Where will the unbelieving, the abominable, murderers, the sexually immoral, sorcerers, and idolaters be placed? C) lake burning with fire and brimstone

📖 REVELATION 21:9–15

Pre-Quiz

1. How many gates did John see on the new, holy Jerusalem?
   A. an uncountable number
   B. twelve
   C. 144,000

2. What names were inscribed on the gates?
   A. the same names in the Book of Life
   B. Father, Son, and Holy Spirit
   C. the twelve tribes of the sons of Israel

3. What was used to measure the city, its gates, and its wall?
   A. the flight of doves
   B. a gold reed
   C. a line of cubits

What the Scriptures Say (Revelation 21:9–15)

Then one of the seven angels who had the seven bowls filled with the seven last plagues came to me and talked with me, saying, "Come, I will show you the bride, the Lamb's wife." And he carried me away in the Spirit to a great and high mountain, and showed me the great city, the holy Jerusalem, descending out of heaven from God, having the glory of God. Her light was like a most precious stone, like a jasper stone, clear as crystal. Also she had a great and high wall with twelve gates, and twelve angels at the gates, and names written on them, which are the names of the twelve tribes of the children of Israel: three gates on the east, three gates on the north, three gates on the south, and three gates on the west. Now the wall of the city had twelve foundations, and on them were the names of the twelve apostles of the Lamb. And he who talked with me had a gold reed to measure the city, its gates, and its wall.

What Revelation 21:9–15 Means

New Jerusalem is described as the Lamb's wife. The greatest feature of the holy city is the illuminating brilliance of God's presence. The book of Ezekiel discusses how glory departed the old Jerusalem and is restored to the New Jerusalem in later times. These are the later times.

Both Jewish and Gentile believers will share in the glory of God through all eternity. Verses 12–14 mentions the names of the twelve tribes of Israel along with the twelve apostles within the gates of the city. This indicates both Jews and Gentiles are present, with the qualifying trait of them all believing in and following Jesus Christ.

He who talked with John had a gold reed to measure the new city.

Revelation 21:9–15 Quiz Answers

1. How many gates did John see on the new, holy Jerusalem? B) twelve
2. What names were inscribed on the gates? C) the twelve tribes of the sons of Israel
3. What was used to measure the city, its gates, and its wall?
   B) a gold reed

📖 REVELATION 21:16–21

Pre-Quiz

1. The length and the breadth and the height of the city are
   A. square
   B. equal
   C. twelve thousand cubics

2. The foundations of the wall of the city had been adorned with
   A. gold
   B. various precious stones
   C. jasper and sapphire

3. The street of the city was pure gold, as
   A. clear glass
   B. ice
   C. molten lava

What the Scriptures Say (Revelation 21:16–21)

The city is laid out as a square; its length is as great as its breadth. And he measured the city with the reed: twelve thousand furlongs. Its length, breadth, and height are equal. Then he measured its wall: one hundred and forty-four cubits, according to the measure of a man, that is, of an angel. The construction of its wall was of jasper; and the city was pure gold, like clear glass. The foundations of the wall of the city were adorned with all kinds of precious stones: the first foundation was jasper, the second sapphire, the third chalcedony, the fourth emerald, the fifth sardonyx, the sixth sardius, the seventh chrysolite, the eighth beryl, the ninth topaz, the tenth chrysoprase, the eleventh jacinth, and the twelfth amethyst. The twelve gates were twelve pearls: each individual gate was of one pearl. And the street of the city was pure gold, like transparent glass.

What Revelation 21:16–21 Means

Once measured, the size of the city is discovered to be approximately fifteen hundred miles long. This is a distance that could cover the eastern seaboard of the United States to the Mississippi River on one side and then stretch from the Canadian border to the Gulf of Mexico on the other side. Additionally, the city will be fifteen hundred miles tall. The vastness and enormity of the city will provide ample space for a vast multitude of saints for all eternity.

Each gate to the city will contain one pearl that is large enough to cover the gateway to the city. "Pure gold, like clear glass" is the material of the streets. Inhabitants of the great city will actually walk on precious gems.

Revelation 21:16–21 Quiz Answers

1. The length and the breadth and the height of the city are B) equal.
2. The foundations of the wall of the city had been adorned with B) various precious stones.
3. The street of the city was pure gold, as A) clear glass.

📖 REVELATION 21:22–27

Pre-Quiz

1. The city had no need for the sun, because it was illuminated by
   A. the moon
   B. the glory of God
   C. the heavenly stars

2. The gates of the city
   A. only close at night
   B. never close because there is no night
   C. are sealed shut

3. Who will be in the city?
   A. only those who are written in the Lamb's Book of Life
   B. only those who persevered
   C. only those who escaped the Rapture

What the Scriptures Say (Revelation 21:22–27)

But I saw no temple in it, for the Lord God Almighty and the Lamb are its temple. The city had no need of the sun or of the moon to shine in it, for the glory of God illuminated it. The Lamb is its light. And the nations of those who are saved shall walk in its light, and the kings of the earth bring their glory and honor into it. Its gates shall not be shut at all by day (there shall be no night there). And they shall bring the glory and the honor of the nations into it. But there shall by no means enter it anything that defiles, or causes an abomination or a lie, but only those who are written in the Lamb's Book of Life.

What Revelation 21:22–27 Means

There will be no temple in the new holy city. Temples are man's way of having fellowship with God, but now, man will fellowship with God directly, making temples obsolete.

There will be no sin there. Jesus' sacrifice for sin is eternal and does not expire. God and the Lamb are the symbolic temple of the new city.

There will be no need for a sun or moon in the new city, as God's magnificence provides more than enough light. The glory of the Lord will shine and light the entire city. There will no longer be such things as night or darkness, only glorious light of a kind that humans have never experienced before.

Verse 27 again references the "Book of Life." This verse emphasizes that Christ not only knows the heart of each of His believers, but He indeed knows each believer by name.

Revelation 21:22–27 Quiz Answers

1. The city had no need for the sun, because it was illuminated by B) the glory of God.

2. The gates of the city B) never close because there is no night.

3. Who will be in the city? A) only those who are written in the Lamb's Book of Life

REVELATION

22

INSIDE THE GLORIOUS CITY

📖 **REVELATION 22:1–8**

Pre-Quiz

1. What was in the middle of the street?
   A. the throne of God
   B. the tree of life
   C. a river of gold

2. What were the leaves of the tree of life used for?
   A. healing the nations
   B. feeding the nations
   C. sanctifying the nations

3. When John saw and heard those things, he fell down to worship before the feet of
   A. the angel showing him those things
   B. Jesus
   C. the four elders

What the Scriptures Say (Revelation 22:1–8)

And he showed me a pure river of water of life, clear as crystal, proceeding from the throne of God and of the Lamb. In the middle of its street, and on either side of the river, was the tree of life, which bore twelve fruits, each tree yielding its fruit every month. The leaves of the tree were for the healing of the nations. And there shall be no more curse, but the throne of God and of the Lamb shall be in it, and His servants shall serve Him. They shall see His face, and His name shall be on their foreheads. There shall be no night there: They need no lamp nor light of the sun, for the Lord God gives them light. And they shall reign forever and ever. Then he said to me, "These words are faithful and true."

And the Lord God of the holy prophets sent His angel to show His servants the things which must shortly take place. "Behold, I am coming quickly! Blessed is he who keeps the words of the prophecy of this book."

Now I, John, saw and heard these things. And when I heard and saw, I fell down to worship before the feet of the angel who showed me these things.

What Revelation 22:1–8 Means

John views a river flowing from the throne of God. It provides the eternal life that flows from our Lord.

The "tree of life" is the same one mentioned in Genesis 3 in which Adam and Eve violated God's command in the garden of Eden. We are told of a complete restoration of Paradise. Everything lost in the fall of man due to the sin committed in the garden is restored. The leaves of the tree of life are used to mend the nations and their relationships toward one another.

Eternal life includes willing servitude to the Lord for all eternity. It is a state of bliss and unspeakable joy. "They shall see His face," indicates that we will have a physical presence with the Lord, and He with us.

"Behold, I am coming quickly!" *Quickly* means "suddenly" in this context. When the saints of Christ are raptured to heaven, Christ will come suddenly, in "the twinkling of an eye" (1 Cor. 15:52).

Terms from the New Testament for the Tribulation

The great Tribulation	Matthew 24:21; Revelation 2:22; 7:14
The Tribulation	Matthew 24:29
The wrath to come	1 Thessalonians 1:10
The day of the Lord	1 Thessalonians 5:2
The wrath	1 Thessalonians 5:9; Revelation 11:18
The hour of trial	Revelation 3:10
The great day of the wrath of the Lamb of God	Revelation 6:16–17
The hour of judgment	Revelation 14:7
The wrath of God	Revelation 14:10,19; 15:1, 7; 16:1

Revelation 22:1–8 Quiz Answers

1. What was in the middle of the street? B) the tree of life
2. What were the leaves of the tree of life used for? A) healing the nations
3. When John saw and heard those things, he fell down to worship before the feet of A) the angel showing him those things.

📖 REVELATION 22:9–16

Pre-Quiz

1. Revelation 22:9 commands us to worship
   A. the throne
   B. the heavens
   C. God

2. Those who do His commandments will
   A. have cups of gold
   B. enter into the city
   C. have the riches of the universe

3. Jesus says that He is the Bright and Morning
   A. Sun
   B. Star
   C. Lamb

What the Scriptures Say (Revelation 22:9–16)

Then he said to me, "See that you do not do that. For I am your fellow servant, and of your brethren the prophets, and of those who keep the words of this book. Worship God." And he said to me, "Do not seal the words of the prophecy of this book, for the time is at hand. He who is unjust, let him be unjust still; he who is filthy, let him be filthy still; he who is righteous, let him be righteous still; he who is holy, let him be holy still. And behold, I am coming quickly, and My reward is with Me, to give to every one according to his work. I am the Alpha and the Omega, the Beginning and the End, the First and the Last."

Blessed are those who do His commandments, that they may have the right to the tree of life, and may enter through the gates into the city. But outside are dogs and sorcerers and sexually immoral and murderers and idolaters, and whoever loves and practices a lie.

"I, Jesus, have sent My angel to testify to you these things in the churches. I am the Root and the Offspring of David, the Bright and Morning Star."

What Revelation 22:9–16 Means

Daniel 12:4 reads: "But you, Daniel, shut up the words, and seal the book until the time of the end." But now the opposite is true as the command is given not to seal the prophetic message, because the time is at hand. The prophecy could not come true until after the death and resurrection of Jesus Christ. Jesus opened the seven seals in Revelation 5–6 to show what would happen in future times, and now the entire book remains open.

In eternity, there will be no second chances for those consigned to the lake of fire. The numerous opportunities to accept Jesus Christ as their Lord and Savior have passed for all time. Once the condemned are judged at the Great White Throne Judgment, they are banished from God's presence forever.

Verse 16 is Christ's stamp of approval on the entire book of Revelation.

Revelation 22:9–16 Quiz Answers

1. Revelation 22:9 commands us to worship C) God.
2. Those who do His commandments will B) enter into the city.
3. Jesus says that He is the Bright and Morning B) Star.

📖 REVELATION 22:17–21

Pre-Quiz

1. If anyone adds to the book, what will happen?
   A. God will add the plagues on him.
   B. God will vomit him out of His mouth.
   C. The writer will perish.

2. Jesus says He is coming
   A. when all the work is gone
   B. when the city is prepared
   C. quickly

3. What is the final word of the book of Revelation?
   A. Christ
   B. soon
   C. Amen

What the Scriptures Say (Revelation 22:17–21)

And the Spirit and the bride say, "Come!" And let him who hears say, "Come!" And let him who thirsts come. Whoever desires, let him take the water of life freely.

For I testify to everyone who hears the words of the prophecy of this book: If anyone adds to these things, God will add to him the plagues that are written in this book; and if anyone takes away from the words of the book of this prophecy, God shall take away his part from the Book of Life, from the holy city, and from the things which are written in this book.

He who testifies to these things says, "Surely I am coming quickly." Amen. Even so, come, Lord Jesus!

The grace of our Lord Jesus Christ be with you all. Amen.

What Revelation 22:17–21 Means

Jesus reemphasizes that the first job for Him and His people is to invite the lost—men, women, and children—to come to Him. He offers salvation before it is too late.

John offers a warning to anyone who "adds to these things" or "takes away" any of the truth of Revelation.

The return of Christ will occur "quickly," or suddenly. There will be no warning or indication of the abruptness of His return. All followers of Christ should eagerly await His return, and as Paul said in 1 Corinthians 16:22, "O Lord, come!"

Ever since the day Jesus ascended to heaven, His Holy Spirit and His church (the bride) have been inviting this lost world to come and drink of the eternal Word of God and its gospel of the kingdom that saves and satisfies the soul in this life and for the eternity He has prepared for us.

And, of course, Jesus our Lord, "the Spirit of prophecy," has blessed you, and will continue to do so, as you share His prophetic Word with your friends and family and know that His ultimate prophecy, "I am coming quickly," means He is coming suddenly. It will be so sudden there will be no time to prepare to meet God. That is why the Bible challenges us if we have any doubt of our salvation that "now is the accepted time; behold, now is the day of salvation" (2 Cor. 6:2). For only you can call on the name of the Lord Jesus Christ in faith and repentance . . . and be saved.

May the grace of our Lord Jesus Christ be with you all.

Revelation 22:17–21 Quiz Answers

1. If anyone adds to the book, what will happen? A) God will add the plagues on him.
2. Jesus says He is coming C) quickly.
3. What is the final word of the book of Revelation? C) Amen

APPENDIX A

WHAT CHRIST SAYS IN REVELATION 1–3 THAT SHOULD BRING US JOY

1:8: "I am the Alpha and the Omega."

1:17: "I am the First and the Last." This speaks of Christ's eternity.

1:18: "I am He who lives, and was dead . . ." This indicates His life on earth and His crucifixion.

1:18: "I am He who lives, and was dead, and behold, I am alive forevermore." This speaks of His resurrection and eternity.

1:18: "And I have the keys of Hades and of Death." Christ controls who goes to hell and the future of all believers.

2:1: "These things says He who holds the seven stars in His right hand." Christ controls the messengers of the churches.

2:1: ". . . who walks in the midst of the seven golden lampstands." Christ walks among the churches, easily accessible to them if they desire.

2:8: "These things says the First and the Last, who was dead, and came to life." Here Christ combines a reference to His eternal nature with the fact of His death and resurrection.

2:11: "He who overcomes shall not be hurt by the second death." Believers will not be "cast into the lake of fire" (Rev. 20:15) but are saved from eternal death, which means eternal separation from God.

2:12: "These things says He who has the sharp two-edged sword."
Christ presents the Word of God as His offensive weapon.

2:17: "To him who overcomes I will give . . . a white stone, and on the
stone a new name written which no one knows except him who
receives it." The stone indicates acquittal from our sins, and just
as Christ renamed Peter and Paul after their conversions, our
new name points to the new life we have in Him.

2:18: ". . . the Son of God." This asserts Christ's relationship to God as
His divine Son.

2:18: ". . . who has eyes like a flame of fire." This is an obvious
reference to His searching gaze on the work of His church.

2:18: ". . . His feet like fine brass." Bronze, or brass, speaks of
judgment. The Lord Jesus Christ will one day judge all people.

2:26–27: "And he who overcomes, and keeps My works until the end,
to him I will give power over the nations—'He shall rule them
with a rod of iron; they shall be dashed to pieces like the potter's
vessels'—as I also have received from My Father." This indicates
that believers will rule and reign with Christ in the Millennium.

2:28: "I will give him the morning star." This is Christ's promise to
come into the believer's heart and dwell with him or her.

3:1: "These things says He who has the seven Spirits of God and the
seven stars." The Holy Spirit will guide the "star" messengers of
the churches. The church has never been without guidance, if she
would look for it.

3:5: "He who overcomes shall be clothed in white garments." The
believer's sinful nature is covered by the righteousness of Christ.

3:5: "I will not blot out his name from the Book of Life." Only those
whose names are not written in the Book of Life are "cast into
the lake of fire." Believers need never fear hell, for Christ will see
that our names remain in His Book of Life.

3:5: ". . . but I will confess his name before My Father and before His
angels." Sinful human beings have no right to go to heaven in the

presence of the Father and His angels; but Jesus will confess our names, thus giving us the right to be there.

3:7: "These things says He who is holy." His nature is holy.

3:7: ". . . is true." His testimony is right and can be relied upon.

3:7: ". . . who has the key of David." Authority to rule over God's people is His.

3:7: "He who opens and no one shuts, and shuts and no one opens." Christ controls our opportunities to serve Him.

3:12: "He who overcomes, I will make him a pillar in the temple of My God, and he shall go out no more." Believers will have access to the Holy Place of God.

3:12: "I will write on him the name of My God and the name of the city of My God, the New Jerusalem, which comes down out of heaven from My God." Believers will be eternally identified with Christ and thus have access to the Holy City, which is to come down from heaven.

3:12: "I will write on him My new name." Believers will be eternally identified with Christ.

3:14: "These things says the Amen." He has final authority.

3:14: ". . . the Faithful and True Witness." He is the revelation of God.

3:14: ". . . the Beginning of the creation of God." Christ is the author and source of all God's creation.

3:20: "Behold, I stand at the door and knock. If anyone hears My voice and opens the door, I will come in to him and dine with him, and he with Me." The Lord of glory pictures Himself standing without, knocking at the door of a person's heart. He does not force His entrance, but leaves it to the individual to invite Him to come in.

3:21: "To him who overcomes I will grant to sit with Me on My throne." Believers will have a share in the ruling of Christ's coming kingdom.

APPENDIX B

NAMES FOR OUR LORD THROUGHOUT SCRIPTURE

Abba (Father) "For you did not receive the spirit of bondage again to fear, but you received the Spirit of adoption by whom we cry out, 'Abba, Father.'" (Romans 8:15)

Advocate "My little children, these things I write to you, so that you may not sin. And if anyone sins, we have an Advocate with the Father, Jesus Christ the righteous." (1 John 2:1)

Almighty "When Abram was ninety-nine years old, the LORD appeared to Abram and said to him, 'I am Almighty God; walk before Me and be blameless.'" (Genesis 17:1)

Alpha "I am the Alpha and the Omega, the Beginning and the End, the First and the Last." (Revelation 22:13)

Ancient of Days "I watched till thrones were put in place, and the Ancient of Days was seated; His garment was white as snow, and the hair of His head was like pure wool. His throne was a fiery flame, its wheels a burning fire." (Daniel 7:9)

Anointed "The kings of the earth set themselves, and the rulers take counsel together, against the LORD and against His Anointed, saying . . ." (Psalm 2:2)

Apostle "Therefore, holy brethren, partakers of the heavenly calling, consider the Apostle and High Priest of our confession, Christ Jesus." (Hebrews 3:1)

Arm of the Lord "Who has believed our report? And to whom has the arm of the LORD been revealed?" (Isaiah 53:1)

Author of Our Faith "Looking unto Jesus, the author and finisher of our faith, who for the joy that was set before Him endured the cross, despising the shame, and has sat down at the right hand of the throne of God." (Hebrews 12:2)

Beginning "And He said to me, 'It is done! I am the Alpha and the Omega, the Beginning and the End. I will give of the fountain of the water of life freely to him who thirsts.'" (Revelation 21:6)

Blessed and Only Potentate "Which He will manifest in His own time, He who is the blessed and only Potentate, the King of kings and Lord of lords." (1 Timothy 6:15)

Branch "In those days and at that time I will cause to grow up to David a Branch of righteousness; He shall execute judgment and righteousness in the earth." (Jeremiah 33:15)

Bread of God "For the bread of God is He who comes down from heaven and gives life to the world." (John 6:33)

Bread of Life "And Jesus said to them, 'I am the bread of life. He who comes to Me shall never hunger, and he who believes in Me shall never thirst.'" (John 6:35)

Bright and Morning Star "I, Jesus, have sent My angel to testify to you these things in the churches. I am the Root and the Offspring of David, the Bright and Morning Star." (Revelation 22:16)

Brightness of God's Glory "Who being the brightness of His glory and the express image of His person, and upholding all things by the word of His power, when He had by Himself purged our sins, sat down at the right hand of the Majesty on high." (Hebrews 1:3)

Chief Shepherd "And when the Chief Shepherd appears, you will receive the crown of glory that does not fade away." (1 Peter 5:4)

Christ "Saying, 'What do you think about the Christ? Whose Son is He?' They said to Him, 'The Son of David.'" (Matthew 22:42)

Christ of God "He said to them, 'But who do you say that I am?' Peter answered and said, 'The Christ of God.'" (Luke 9:20)

Christ the Lord "For there is born to you this day in the city of David a Savior, who is Christ the Lord." (Luke 2:11)

Christ, the Son of the Living God "Simon Peter answered and said, 'You are the Christ, the Son of the living God.'" (Matthew 16:16)

Consolation of Israel "And behold, there was a man in Jerusalem whose name was Simeon, and this man was just and devout, waiting for the Consolation of Israel, and the Holy Spirit was upon him." (Luke 2:25)

Consuming Fire "For the LORD your God is a consuming fire, a jealous God." (Deuteronomy 4:24)

Cornerstone "Therefore thus says the Lord GOD: 'Behold, I lay in Zion a stone for a foundation, a tried stone, a precious cornerstone, a sure foundation; whoever believes will not act hastily." (Isaiah 28:16)

Counselor "For unto us a Child is born, unto us a Son is given; and the government will be upon His shoulder. And His name will be called Wonderful, Counselor, Mighty God, Everlasting Father, Prince of Peace." (Isaiah 9:6)

Creator "Therefore let those who suffer according to the will of God commit their souls to Him in doing good, as to a faithful Creator." (1 Peter 4:19)

Deliverer "And so all Israel will be saved, as it is written: 'The Deliverer will come out of Zion, and He will turn away ungodliness from Jacob.'" (Romans 11:26)

Desire of All Nations "'And I will shake all nations, and they shall come to the Desire of All Nations, and I will fill this temple with glory,' says the LORD of hosts." (Haggai 2:7)

Door "Then Jesus said to them again, 'Most assuredly, I say to you, I am the door of the sheep.'" (John 10:7)

Elect One "Behold! My Servant whom I uphold, My Elect One in whom My soul delights! I have put My Spirit upon Him; He will bring forth justice to the Gentiles." (Isaiah 42:1)

End "And He said to me, 'It is done! I am the Alpha and the Omega, the Beginning and the End. I will give of the fountain of the water of life freely to him who thirsts.'" (Revelation 21:6)

Eternal God "The eternal God is your refuge, and underneath are the everlasting arms; He will thrust out the enemy from before you, and will say, 'Destroy!'" (Deuteronomy 33:27)

Everlasting Father "For unto us a Child is born, unto us a Son is given; and the government will be upon His shoulder. And His name will be called Wonderful, Counselor, Mighty God, Everlasting Father, Prince of Peace." (Isaiah 9:6)

Faithful and True "Now I saw heaven opened, and behold, a white horse. And He who sat on him was called Faithful and True, and in righteousness He judges and makes war." (Revelation 19:11)

Faithful Witness "And from Jesus Christ, the faithful witness, the firstborn from the dead, and the ruler over the kings of the earth. To Him who loved us and washed us from our sins in His own blood." (Revelation 1:5)

Father "In this manner, therefore, pray: Our Father in heaven, hallowed be Your name." (Matthew 6:9)

Firstfruits "But now Christ is risen from the dead, and has become the firstfruits of those who have fallen asleep." (1 Corinthians 15:20)

Foundation "For no other foundation can anyone lay than that which is laid, which is Jesus Christ." (1 Corinthians 3:11)

Friend of Tax Collectors and Sinners "The Son of Man came eating and drinking, and they say, 'Look, a glutton and a winebibber, a friend of tax collectors and sinners!' But wisdom is justified by her children." (Matthew 11:19)

Gift of God "Jesus answered and said to her, 'If you knew the gift of God, and who it is who says to you, "Give Me a drink," you would have asked Him, and He would have given you living water.'" (John 4:10)

God "In the beginning God created the heavens and the earth." (Genesis 1:1)

God over All "Of whom are the fathers and from whom, according to the flesh, Christ came, who is over all, the eternally blessed God. Amen." (Romans 9:5)

God Who Sees "Then she called the name of the LORD who spoke to her, You-Are-the-God-Who-Sees; for she said, 'Have I also here seen Him who sees me?'" (Genesis 16:13)

Good Shepherd "I am the good shepherd. The good shepherd gives His life for the sheep." (John 10:11)

Great High Priest "Seeing then that we have a great High Priest who has passed through the heavens, Jesus the Son of God, let us hold fast our confession." (Hebrews 4:14)

Great Shepherd "Now may the God of peace who brought up our Lord Jesus from the dead, that great Shepherd of the sheep, through the blood of the everlasting covenant." (Hebrews 13:20)

Guide "For this is God, our God forever and ever; He will be our guide even to death." (Psalm 48:14)

Head of the Body "And He is the head of the body, the church, who is the beginning, the firstborn from the dead, that in all things He may have the preeminence." (Colossians 1:18)

Head of the Church "For the husband is head of the wife, as also Christ is head of the church; and He is the Savior of the body." (Ephesians 5:23)

Heir of All Things "Has in these last days spoken to us by His Son, whom He has appointed heir of all things, through whom also He made the worlds." (Hebrews 1:2)

Helper "But the Helper, the Holy Spirit, whom the Father will send in My name, He will teach you all things, and bring to your remembrance all things that I said to you." (John 14:26)

High Priest "Therefore, holy brethren, partakers of the heavenly calling, consider the Apostle and High Priest of our confession, Christ Jesus." (Hebrews 3:1)

High Priest Forever "Where the forerunner has entered for us, even Jesus, having become High Priest forever according to the order of Melchizedek." (Hebrews 6:20)

Holy One "For You will not leave my soul in Hades, nor will You allow Your Holy One to see corruption." (Acts 2:27)

Holy One of Israel "Thus says the LORD, the Redeemer of Israel, their Holy One, to Him whom man despises, to Him whom the nation abhors, to the Servant of rulers: 'Kings shall see and arise, princes also shall worship, because of the Lord who is faithful, the Holy One of Israel; and He has chosen You.'" (Isaiah 49:7)

Holy Spirit "In that day you will ask in my name, and I do not say to you that I shall pray to the Father for you." (John 16:26)

Hope "Looking for the blessed hope and glorious appearing of our great God and Savior Jesus Christ." (Titus 2:13)

Horn of Salvation "And has raised up a horn of salvation for us in the house of His servant David." (Luke 1:69)

I Am "And God said to Moses, 'I AM WHO I AM.' And He said, 'Thus you shall say to the children of Israel, "I AM has sent me to you."'" (Exodus 3:14)

Image of God "Whose minds the god of this age has blinded, who do not believe, lest the light of the gospel of the glory of Christ, who is the image of God, should shine on them." (2 Corinthians 4:4)

Image of His Person "Who being the brightness of His glory and the express image of His person, and upholding all things by the word of His power, when He had by Himself purged our sins, sat down at the right hand of the Majesty on high." (Hebrews 1:3)

Immanuel "Therefore the Lord Himself will give you a sign: Behold, the virgin shall conceive and bear a Son, and shall call His name Immanuel." (Isaiah 7:14)

Jealous "For you shall worship no other god, for the Lord, whose name is Jealous, is a jealous God." (Exodus 34:14)

Jehovah "That they may know that You, whose name alone is the Lord, are the Most High over all the earth." (Psalm 83:18)

Jesus "And she will bring forth a Son, and you shall call His name Jesus, for He will save His people from their sins." (Matthew 1:21)

Jesus Christ Our Lord "For the wages of sin is death, but the gift of God is eternal life in Christ Jesus our Lord." (Romans 6:23)

Judge "For the Lord is our Judge, the Lord is our Lawgiver, the Lord is our King; He will save us." (Isaiah 33:22)

King "Rejoice greatly, O daughter of Zion! Shout, O daughter of Jerusalem! Behold, your King is coming to you; He is just and having salvation, lowly and riding on a donkey, a colt, the foal of a donkey." (Zechariah 9:9)

King Eternal "Now to the King eternal, immortal, invisible, to God who alone is wise, be honor and glory forever and ever. Amen." (1 Timothy 1:17)

King of kings "Which He will manifest in His own time, He who is the blessed and only Potentate, the King of kings and Lord of lords." (1 Timothy 6:15)

King of the Saints "They sing the song of Moses, the servant of God, and the song of the Lamb, saying: 'Great and marvelous are Your works, Lord God Almighty! Just and true are Your ways, O King of the saints!'" (Revelation 15:3)

Lamb of God "The next day John saw Jesus coming toward him, and said, 'Behold! The Lamb of God who takes away the sin of the world!'" (John 1:29)

Last Adam "And so it is written, 'The first man Adam became a living being.' The last Adam became a life-giving spirit." (1 Corinthians 15:45)

Lawgiver "For the Lord is our Judge, the Lord is our Lawgiver, the Lord is our King; He will save us." (Isaiah 33:22)

Leader "Indeed I have given him as a witness to the people, a leader and commander for the people." (Isaiah 55:4)

Life "Jesus said to him, 'I am the way, the truth, and the life. No one comes to the Father except through Me.'" (John 14:6)

Light of the World "Then Jesus spoke to them again, saying, 'I am the light of the world. He who follows Me shall not walk in darkness, but have the light of life.'" (John 8:12)

Lily of the Valleys "I am the rose of Sharon, and the lily of the valleys." (Song of Solomon 2:1)

Lion of the Tribe of Judah "But one of the elders said to me, 'Do not weep. Behold, the Lion of the tribe of Judah, the Root of David, has prevailed to open the scroll and to loose its seven seals.'" (Revelation 5:5)

Living Stone "Coming to Him as to a living stone, rejected indeed by men, but chosen by God and precious." (1 Peter 2:4)

Living Water "Jesus answered and said to her, 'If you knew the gift of God, and who it is who says to you, "Give Me a drink," you would have asked Him, and He would have given you living water.'" (John 4:10)

Lord "You call Me Teacher and Lord, and you say well, for so I am." (John 13:13)

Lord God Almighty "They sing the song of Moses, the servant of God, and the song of the Lamb, saying: 'Great and marvelous are Your works, Lord God Almighty! Just and true are Your ways, O King of the saints!'" (Revelation 15:3)

Lord Jesus Christ "But thanks be to God, who gives us the victory through our Lord Jesus Christ." (1 Corinthians 15:57)

Lord of All "The word which God sent to the children of Israel, preaching peace through Jesus Christ—He is Lord of all." (Acts 10:36)

Lord of Glory "Which none of the rulers of this age knew; for had they known, they would not have crucified the Lord of glory." (1 Corinthians 2:8)

Lord of lords "Which He will manifest in His own time, He who is the blessed and only Potentate, the King of kings and Lord of lords." (1 Timothy 6:15)

Lord Our Righteousness "In His days Judah will be saved, and Israel will dwell safely; now this is His name by which He will be called: THE LORD OUR RIGHTEOUSNESS." (Jeremiah 23:6)

Love "He who does not love does not know God, for God is love." (1 John 4:8)

Man of Sorrows "He is despised and rejected by men, a Man of sorrows and acquainted with grief. And we hid, as it were, our faces from Him; He was despised, and we did not esteem Him." (Isaiah 53:3)

Master "But Simon answered and said to Him, 'Master, we have toiled all night and caught nothing; nevertheless at Your word I will let down the net.'" (Luke 5:5)

Mediator "For there is one God and one Mediator between God and men, the Man Christ Jesus." (1 Timothy 2:5)

Merciful God "Go and proclaim these words toward the north, and say: 'Return, backsliding Israel,' says the Lord; 'I will not cause My anger to fall on you. For I am merciful,' says the Lord; 'I will not remain angry forever.'" (Jeremiah 3:12)

Messenger of the Covenant "'Behold, I send My messenger, and he will prepare the way before Me. And the Lord, whom you seek, will suddenly come to His temple, even the Messenger of the covenant, in whom you delight. Behold, He is coming,' says the Lord of hosts." (Malachi 3:1)

Messiah "The woman said to Him, 'I know that Messiah is coming' (who is called Christ). 'When He comes, He will tell us all things.'" (John 4:25)

Mighty God "For unto us a Child is born, unto us a Son is given; and the government will be upon His shoulder. And His name will be called Wonderful, Counselor, Mighty God, Everlasting Father, Prince of Peace." (Isaiah 9:6)

Mighty One "You shall drink the milk of the Gentiles, and milk the breast of kings; you shall know that I, the Lord, am your Savior and your Redeemer, the Mighty One of Jacob." (Isaiah 60:16)

Nazarene "And he came and dwelt in a city called Nazareth, that it might be fulfilled which was spoken by the prophets, 'He shall be called a Nazarene.'" (Matthew 2:23)

Offspring of David "I, Jesus, have sent My angel to testify to you these things in the churches. I am the Root and the Offspring of David, the Bright and Morning Star." (Revelation 22:16)

Only Begotten Son "No one has seen God at any time. The only begotten Son, who is in the bosom of the Father, He has declared Him." (John 1:18)

Our Passover Lamb "Therefore purge out the old leaven, that you may be a new lump, since you truly are unleavened. For indeed Christ, our Passover, was sacrificed for us." (1 Corinthians 5:7)

Our Peace "For He Himself is our peace, who has made both one, and has broken down the middle wall of separation." (Ephesians 2:14)

Potter "But now, O LORD, You are our Father; we are the clay, and You our potter; and all we are the work of Your hand." (Isaiah 64:8)

Power of God "But to those who are called, both Jews and Greeks, Christ the power of God and the wisdom of God." (1 Corinthians 1:24)

Prince of Life "And killed the Prince of life, whom God raised from the dead, of which we are witnesses." (Acts 3:15)

Prince of Peace "For unto us a Child is born, unto us a Son is given; and the government will be upon His shoulder. And His name will be called Wonderful, Counselor, Mighty God, Everlasting Father, Prince of Peace." (Isaiah 9:6)

Prophet "For Moses truly said to the fathers, 'The LORD your God will raise up for you a Prophet like me from your brethren. Him you shall hear in all things, whatever He says to you.'" (Acts 3:22)

Purifier "He will sit as a refiner and a purifier of silver; He will purify the sons of Levi, and purge them as gold and silver, that they may offer to the LORD an offering in righteousness." (Malachi 3:3)

Rabboni (Teacher) "Jesus said to her, 'Mary!' She turned and said to Him, 'Rabboni!' (which is to say, Teacher)." (John 20:16)

Redeemer "For I know that my Redeemer lives, and He shall stand at last on the earth." (Job 19:25)

Refiner's Fire "But who can endure the day of His coming? And who can stand when He appears? For He is like a refiner's fire and like launderers' soap." (Malachi 3:2)

Resurrection "Jesus said to her, 'I am the resurrection and the life. He who believes in Me, though he may die, he shall live.'" (John 11:25)

Righteous One "My little children, these things I write to you, so that you may not sin. And if anyone sins, we have an Advocate with the Father, Jesus Christ the righteous." (1 John 2:1)

Rock "And all drank the same spiritual drink. For they drank of that spiritual Rock that followed them, and that Rock was Christ." (1 Corinthians 10:4)

Root of David "I, Jesus, have sent My angel to testify to you these things in the churches. I am the Root and the Offspring of David, the Bright and Morning Star." (Revelation 22:16)

Rose of Sharon "I am the rose of Sharon, and the lily of the valleys." (Song of Solomon 2:1)

Ruler in Israel "But you, Bethlehem Ephrathah, though you are little among the thousands of Judah, yet out of you shall come forth to Me the One to be Ruler in Israel, whose goings forth are from of old, from everlasting." (Micah 5:2)

Ruler of God's Creation "And to the angel of the church of the Laodiceans write, 'These things says the Amen, the Faithful and True Witness, the Beginning of the creation of God.'" (Revelation 3:14)

Ruler over the Kings of the Earth "And from Jesus Christ, the faithful witness, the firstborn from the dead, and the ruler over the kings of the earth. To Him who loved us and washed us from our sins in His own blood." (Revelation 1:5)

Savior "For there is born to you this day in the city of David a Savior, who is Christ the Lord." (Luke 2:11)

Scepter out of Israel "I see Him, but not now; I behold Him, but not near; a Star shall come out of Jacob; a Scepter shall rise out of Israel, and batter the brow of Moab, and destroy all the sons of tumult." (Numbers 24:17)

Seed "And I will put enmity between you and the woman, and between your seed and her Seed; He shall bruise your head, and you shall bruise His heel." (Genesis 3:15)

Servant "Behold! My Servant whom I uphold, My Elect One in whom My soul delights! I have put My Spirit upon Him; He will bring forth justice to the Gentiles." (Isaiah 42:1)

Shepherd of Our Souls "For you were like sheep going astray, but have now returned to the Shepherd and Overseer of your souls." (1 Peter 2:25)

Shield "After these things the word of the LORD came to Abram in a vision, saying, 'Do not be afraid, Abram. I am your shield, your exceedingly great reward.'"(Genesis 15:1)

Son of David "The book of the genealogy of Jesus Christ, the Son of David, the Son of Abraham." (Matthew 1:1)

Son of God "So when the centurion and those with him, who were guarding Jesus, saw the earthquake and the things that had happened, they feared greatly, saying, 'Truly this was the Son of God!'" (Matthew 27:54)

Son of Man "And Jesus said to him, 'Foxes have holes and birds of the air have nests, but the Son of Man has nowhere to lay His head.'" (Matthew 8:20)

Son of the Highest "He will be great, and will be called the Son of the Highest; and the Lord God will give Him the throne of His father David." (Luke 1:32)

Source "And having been perfected, He became the author of eternal salvation to all who obey Him." (Hebrews 5:9)

Spirit of God "The earth was without form, and void; and darkness was on the face of the deep. And the Spirit of God was hovering over the face of the waters." (Genesis 1:2)

Star out of Jacob "I see Him, but not now; I behold Him, but not near; a Star shall come out of Jacob; a Scepter shall rise out of Israel, and batter the brow of Moab, and destroy all the sons of tumult." (Numbers 24:17)

Still Small Voice "And after the earthquake a fire; but the LORD was not in the fire; and after the fire a still small voice." (1 Kings 19:12)

Stone "And 'a stone of stumbling and a rock of offense.' They stumble, being disobedient to the word, to which they also were appointed." (1 Peter 2:8)

Sun of Righteousness "But to you who fear My name the Sun of Righteousness shall arise with healing in His wings; and you shall go out and grow fat like stall-fed calves." (Malachi 4:2)

Teacher "You call Me Teacher and Lord, and you say well, for so I am." (John 13:13)

True Light "That was the true Light which gives light to every man coming into the world." (John 1:9)

True Witness "And to the angel of the church of the Laodiceans write, 'These things says the Amen, the Faithful and True Witness, the Beginning of the creation of God.'" (Revelation 3:14)

Truth "Jesus said to him, 'I am the way, the truth, and the life. No one comes to the Father except through Me.'" (John 14:6)

Vine "I am the vine, you are the branches. He who abides in Me, and I in him, bears much fruit; for without Me you can do nothing." (John 15:5)

Way "Jesus said to him, 'I am the way, the truth, and the life. No one comes to the Father except through Me.'" (John 14:6)

Wisdom of God "But to those who are called, both Jews and Greeks, Christ the power of God and the wisdom of God." (1 Corinthians 1:24)

Witness "Indeed I have given him as a witness to the people, a leader and commander for the people." (Isaiah 55:4)

Wonderful "For unto us a Child is born, unto us a Son is given; and the government will be upon His shoulder. And His name will be called Wonderful, Counselor, Mighty God, Everlasting Father, Prince of Peace." (Isaiah 9:6)

Word "In the beginning was the Word, and the Word was with God, and the Word was God." (John 1:1)

Word of God "He was clothed with a robe dipped in blood, and His name is called The Word of God." (Revelation 19:13)

About the Authors

Dr. Tim LaHaye is president of Tim LaHaye Ministries and founder of the Pre-Trib Research Center. He has written more than sixty nonfiction books, and his writings are best noted for their easy-to-understand and scripturally based application of biblical principles that assist in facing and handling the challenges of life.

In the fiction arena, it was Tim LaHaye who originated the idea of a novel about the second coming of Christ. His Left Behind series, written with Jerry Jenkins, has been the fastest-selling Christian fiction series ever, with more than seventy million copies sold.

Dr. LaHaye holds the Doctor of Ministry degree from Western Theological Seminary and the Doctor of Literature degree from Liberty University. He and his wife, Beverly, have been married more than sixty-five years. She is founder and chairman of the board of Concerned Women for America. Together they have four children, nine grandchildren, and thirteen great-grandchildren.

Puzzle master Timothy E. Parker is senior crossword puzzle editor of *USA Today* crosswords and the "World's Most Syndicated Puzzle Compiler" according to *Guinness World Records*. In 1997 he taught himself computer programming and created the first interactive crossword for the Internet. His creation, the Universal Crossword, is syndicated around the world, in print and online.

In 1999, Parker founded the Puzzle Society, one of North America's largest paid-subscriber puzzle clubs. The club has become so popular, the *Washington Post* crosswords, *Los Angeles Times* crosswords, Jumble, and *USA Today* crosswords offer puzzles through Parker's club.

Parker is the author of *King James Games*, a puzzle book that teaches Scripture, and more than a dozen puzzle books and primers.

Parker is the founder of Bible Brilliant, a company formed to teach scriptures using the Bible, not doctrine, as the guide for learning.

Parker is an alumnus of the prestigious Gilman School and lives in Ellicott City, Maryland, with his wife, evangelist Giselle Parker, and his two children, Timothy Jr. and Brooke.